IBM

NETeam

Building a Stronger

Business Connection

This book belongs to:

_____

Bartlett's Book of Business Quotations

Bartlett's Book of Business Quotations

Compiled by Barbara Ann Kipfer

LITTLE, BROWN AND COMPANY

BOSTON   NEW YORK   TORONTO   LONDON

First Edition

Illustrations by Carol O'Malia

Library of Congress Cataloging-in-Publication Data

Bartlett's book of business quotations / compiled by Barbara Ann
  Kipfer. — 1st ed.
      p.   cm.
  A thematic grouping of quotations from: Familiar quotations /
[compiled by] John Bartlett.
  ISBN 0-316-08291-0
  1. Business — Quotations, maxims, etc. I. Bartlett, John,
1820–1905. II. Kipfer, Barbara Ann. III. Title: Book of business
quotations.
PN6084.B87B37 1994
650 — dc20   93-29997

10 9 8 7 6 5 4 3 2

BP

*Published simultaneously in Canada
by Little, Brown & Company (Canada) Limited*

Printed in the United States of America

Contents

Entrepreneurship

A teacher affects eternity; he can never tell where his influence stops.

> Henry Adams
> *The Education of Henry Adams* [1907], ch. 20

A pen is certainly an excellent instrument to fix a man's attention and to inflame his ambition.

> John Adams
> Diary [November 14, 1760]

Even when laws have been written down, they ought not always to remain unaltered.

> Aristotle
> *Politics*, bk. II, ch. 8

Every science and every inquiry, and similarly every activity and pursuit, is thought to aim at some good.

> Aristotle
> *Nicomachean Ethics*, bk. I, ch. 1

The two qualities which chiefly inspire regard and affection [are] that a thing is your own and that it is your only one.

> Aristotle
> *Politics*, bk. II, ch. 4

The critical power . . . tends, at last, to make an intellectual situation of which the creative power can profitably avail itself . . . to make the best ideas prevail.

> Arnold
> *The Function of Criticism at the Present Time* [1864]

One of the greatest pains to human nature is the pain of a new idea.

> Walter Bagehot
> *Physics and Politics* [1869], ch. 5

It is a very great thing to be able to think as you like; but, after all, an important question remains: *what* you think.

> Matthew Arnold
> *Democracy* [1861]

He that will not apply new remedies must expect new evils; for time is the greatest innovator.

> Francis Bacon
> *Essays* [1625]. Of Innovations

One's religion is whatever he is most interested in, and yours is Success.

> Sir James M. Barrie
> *The Twelve-Pound Look* [1910]

To be a great man and a saint for
oneself, that is the one important
thing.

> Charles Baudelaire
> *Mon Coeur mis à nu* [1887], LII

It is always good
When a man has two irons in the fire.

> Francis Beaumont and John Fletcher
> *The Faithful Friends* [c. 1608],
> act I, sc. ii

It took me fifteen years to discover
that I had no talent for writing,
but I couldn't give it up because
by that time I was too famous.

> Robert Benchley
> Remark

Of all the ways of acquiring books,
writing them oneself is regarded
as the most praiseworthy
method. . . . Writers are really
people who write books not because they are poor, but because
they are dissatisfied with the
books which they could buy but
do not like.

> Walter Benjamin
> *Unpacking My Library* [1931]

The celebrity is a person who is known for his well-knownness.

> Daniel Boorstin
> *The Image* [1962], ch. 1

Public life is regarded as the crown of a career, and to young men it is the worthiest ambition. Politics is still the greatest and the most honorable adventure.

> John Buchan
> *Pilgrim's Way* [1940]

You can never plan the future by the past.

> Edmund Burke
> Letter to a member
>   of the National Assembly [1791]

An expert is one who knows more and more about less and less.

> Nicholas Murray Butler
> Commencement address, Columbia
>   University

All work, even cotton spinning, is noble; work is alone noble. . . . A life of ease is not for any man, nor for any god.

> Thomas Carlyle
> *Past and Present* [1843], bk. III, ch. 4

He who first shortened the labor of
copyists by device of movable
types was disbanding hired
armies, and cashiering most kings
and senates, and creating a whole
new democratic world: he had
invented the art of printing.

> Carlyle
> *Sartor Resartus* [1833–1834],
> bk. I, ch. 5

Three generations from shirtsleeves
to shirtsleeves.

> Andrew Carnegie
> *Triumphant Democracy* [1886]

"There's no use trying," she said:
"one *can't* believe impossible
things."
"I daresay you haven't had much
practice," said the Queen. "When
I was your age, I always did it for
half-an-hour a day. Why, sometimes I've believed as many as six
impossible things before break-
fast."

> Lewis Carroll
> *Through the Looking-Glass* [1872],
> ch. 5

Thou hast seen nothing yet.

> Miguel de Cervantes
> *Don Quixote de la Mancha,*
> pt. I [l605], bk. III, ch. 11

I feel more confident and more satisfied when I reflect that I have two professions and not one. Medicine is my lawful wife and literature is my mistress. When I get tired of one I spend the night with the other. Though it's disorderly it's not so dull, and besides, neither really loses anything through my infidelity.

> Anton Chekhov
> Letter to A. S. Suvorin
> [September 11, 1888]

The whole difference between construction and creation is exactly this: that a thing constructed can only be loved after it is constructed; but a thing created is loved before it exists.

> G. K. Chesterton
> Preface to Charles Dickens,
> *The Pickwick Papers*

Nothing is more dangerous than an idea, when it's the only one we have.

> Emile Auguste Chartier [Alain]
> *Libres-propos*

Knowledge may give weight, but accomplishments give luster, and many more people see than weigh.

> Philip Dormer Stanhope, Earl of Chesterfield
> *Letters to His Son* [1774]. May 8, 1750

I don't think necessity is the mother of invention — invention, in my opinion, arises directly from idleness, possibly also from laziness. To save oneself trouble.

Agatha Christie
An Autobiography [1977].
Pt. III, Growing Up

It is better to be making the news than taking it; to be an actor rather than a critic.

Winston Churchill
The Malakand Field Force [1898]

This business will never hold water.

Colley Cibber
She Wou'd and She Wou'd Not [1703],
act IV

Imitation is the sincerest of flattery.

Charles Caleb Colton
Lacon [1820–1822], vol. 1, no. 217

There is only one proved method of assisting the advancement of pure science — that of picking men of genius, backing them heavily, and leaving them to direct themselves.

James Bryant Conant
Letter to the *New York Times*
[August 13, 1945]

I owe my fame only to myself.

> Pierre Corneille
> *Poésies diverses,* 23

I love fools' experiments. I am always making them.

> Charles Darwin
> From *Life and Letters of*
>   *Charles Darwin* [1887],
>   edited by Sir Francis Darwin

I want to be something so much worthier than the doll in the doll's house.

> Charles Dickens
> *Our Mutual Friend* [1864–1865],
>   bk. I, ch. 55

This is the thing that I was born to do.

> Samuel Daniel
> *Musophilus* [1599], st. 100

But in science the credit goes to the man who convinces the world, not to the man to whom the idea first occurs.

> Sir Francis Darwin
> First Galton Lecture before
>   the Eugenics Society [1914]

"Hope" is the thing with feathers —
That perches in the soul —
And sings the tune without the words —
And never stops — at all —

> Emily Dickinson
> No. 254 [c. 1861], st. 1

A precedent embalms a principle.

> Benjamin Disraeli
> Speech on the expenditures
>   of the country [February 22, 1848]

Little things affect little minds.

> Disraeli
> *Sybil; or, The Two Nations* [1845],
>   bk. III, ch. 2

It's them that take advantage that
get advantage i' this world.

> George Eliot
> *Adam Bede* [1859], ch. 32

Duty cannot exist without faith.

> Disraeli
> *Tancred* [1847], bk. II, ch. 1

Man is not the creature of circumstances. Circumstances are the
creatures of men.

> Disraeli
> *Vivian Grey* [1826], bk. VI, ch. 7

Genius has no taste for weaving
sand.

> Ralph Waldo Emerson
> *Lectures and Biographical Sketches*
>   [1883]. The Scholar.

I trust a good deal to common fame, as we all must. If a man has good corn, or wood, or boards, or pigs, to sell, or can make better chairs or knives, crucibles or church organs, than anybody else, you will find a broad hard-beaten road to his house, though it be in the woods.

> Emerson
> *Journal.* February 1855

It is the lone worker who makes the first advance in a subject: the details may be worked out by a team, but the prime idea is due to the enterprise, thought and perception of an individual.

> Sir Alexander Fleming
> Address at Edinburgh University
> [1951]

Really the writer doesn't want success. . . . He knows he has a short span of life, that the day will come when he must pass through the wall of oblivion, and he wants to leave a scratch on that wall — Kilroy was here — that somebody a hundred, or a thousand years later will see.

> William Faulkner
> From *Faulkner in the University* [1959],
> Session 8

To know is nothing at all; to imagine is everything.

> Anatole France
> *The Crime of Sylvestre Bonnard* [1881],
> pt. II, ch. 2

Weariness! Weariness! This was life — my life — my career, my brilliant career! I was fifteen — fifteen! A few fleeting hours and I would be as old as those around me.

> Miles Franklin
> *My Brilliant Career* [1901], ch. 5

Originality is something that is easily exaggerated, especially by authors contemplating their own work.

> John Kenneth Galbraith
> *The Affluent Society* [1958], ch. 1

You cannot fight against the future. Time is on our side.

> William Gladstone
> Speech on the Reform Bill [1866]

No idea is so antiquated that it was not once modern. No idea is so modern that it will not someday be antiquated.

> Ellen Glasgow
> Address to the Modern Language
> Association [1936]

Create, artist! Do not talk!

> Johann Wolfgang von Goethe
> Saying

A talent is formed in stillness, a character in the world's torrent.

Goethe
Torquato Tasso [1790], act I, sc. ii

Art is long, life short; judgment difficult, opportunity transient.

Goethe
Wilhelm Meister's Apprenticeship
[1786–1830], bk. VII, ch. 9

Of freedom and of life he only is deserving
Who every day must conquer them anew.

Goethe
Faust. The Second Part [1832],
act V, Court of the Palace

A teacher who can arouse a feeling for one single good action, for one single good poem, accomplishes more than he who fills our memory with rows on rows of natural objects, classified with name and form.

Goethe
Elective Affinities [1808], bk. II, ch. 7

If I work incessantly to the last, nature owes me another form of existence when the present one collapses.

Goethe
Letter to Johann Peter Eckermann
[February 4, 1829]

Individuality of expression is the beginning and end of all art.

> Goethe
> *Proverbs in Prose*

The best business you can go into you will find on your father's farm or in his workshop. If you have no family or friends to aid you, and no prospect opened to you there, turn your face to the great West, and there build up a home and fortune.

> Horace Greeley
> From James Parton,
>   *Life of Horace Greeley* [1855].
>   To Aspiring Young Men

The artist may be well advised to keep his work to himself till it is completed, because no one can readily help him or advise him with it . . . but the scientist is wiser not to withhold a single finding or a single conjecture from publicity.

> Goethe
> *Essay on Experimentation*

Men of genius do not excel in any profession because they labor in it, but they labor in it because they excel.

> William Hazlitt
> *Characteristics,* no. 416 [c. 1821]

Serious occupation is labor that has reference to some want.

> Georg Wilhelm Friedrich Hegel
> *Philosophy of History* [1832], pt. I,
> sec. 2, ch. 1

What makes men happy is liking what they have to do. This is a principle on which society is not founded.

> Claude Adrien Helvétius
> *De l'Esprit* [1758], preface

If a man insisted always on being serious, and never allowed himself a bit of fun and relaxation, he would go mad or become unstable without knowing it.

> Herodotus
> Ibid. bk. II, ch. 173

No author is a man of genius to his publisher.

> Heinrich Heine
> Attributed

Great deeds are usually wrought at great risks.

> Herodotus
> *The Histories of Herodotus,*
> bk. VII, ch. 50

Look ere ye leap.

> Heywood
> Ibid. ch. 2.

I say to you in all sadness of conviction, that to think great thoughts you must be heroes as well as idealists.

> Oliver Wendell Holmes, Jr.
> *The Profession of the Law* [1886]

A councilor ought not to sleep the whole night through, a man to whom the populace is entrusted, and who has many responsibilities.

> Homer
> *The Iliad*, bk. II, l. 24

A hard beginning maketh a good ending.

> John Heywood
> *Proverbs* [1546], pt. 1, ch. 4

A thought is often original, though you have uttered it a hundred times.

> Oliver Wendell Holmes
> *The Autocrat of the Breakfast-Table* [1858], ch. 1

Life is painting a picture, not doing a sum.

> Oliver Wendell Holmes, Jr.
> The Class of '61. From *Speeches* [1913]

Genius is an infinite capacity for taking pains.

> Jane Ellice Hopkins
> *Work Amongst Working Men* [1870]

"Painters and poets," you say, "have always had an equal license in bold invention." We know; we claim the liberty for ourselves and in turn we give it to others.

> Horace
> *Epistles,* bk. III
> (*Ars Poetica*) [c. 8 B.C.], l. 9

That action is best which procures the greatest happiness for the greatest numbers.

> Francis Hutcheson
> *Inquiry Concerning Moral Good and Evil* [1720], sec. 3

The strongest man in the world is he who stands most alone.

> Henrik Ibsen
> *An Enemy of the People* [1882], act V

An invasion of armies can be resisted, but not an idea whose time has come.

> Victor Hugo
> *Histoire d'un crime*
> [written 1852], conclusion

If a little knowledge is dangerous, where is the man who has so much as to be out of danger?

> Thomas Henry Huxley
> *On Elemental Instruction in Physiology* [1877]

What is called a sincere work is one that is endowed with enough strength to give reality to an illusion.

> Max Jacob
> *Art poétique* [1922]

Life being all inclusion and confusion, and art being all discrimination and selection, the latter, in search of the hard latent *value* with which it alone is concerned, sniffs round the mass as instinctively and unerringly as a dog suspicious of some buried bone.

> Henry James
> *Prefaces* [1907–1909].
> *The Spoils of Poynton*

He is no wise man who will quit a certainty for an uncertainty.

> Samuel Johnson
> *The Idler* [1758–1760], no. 57

This world, where much is to be done and little to be known.

> Johnson
> *Prayers and Meditations* [1785].
> Against Inquisitive and Perplexing Thoughts

That one hundred and fifty lawyers should do business together ought not to be expected.

> Thomas Jefferson
> *Autobiography* [January 6, 1821]. On the United States Congress

The applause of a single human being is of great consequence.

> Johnson
> From James Boswell, *Life of Johnson* [1791], 1780

A man of genius makes no mistakes. His errors are volitional and are the portals of discovery.

> James Joyce
> *Ulysses* [1922]

Give me the political economist,
    the sanitary reformer, the engi-
    neer; and take your saints and
    virgins, relics and miracles. The
    spinning-jenny and the railroad,
    Cunard's liners and the electric
    telegraph, are to me . . . signs that
    we are, on some points at least, in
    harmony with the universe.

> Charles Kingsley
> *Yeast* [1848], ch. 5

To produce things and to rear them,
To produce, but not to take posses-
    sion of them,
To act, but not to rely on one's own
    ability,
To lead them, but not to master
    them —
This is called profound and secret
    virtue.

> Lao-tzu
> *The Way of Lao-tzu,* 10

We heed no instincts but our own.

> Jean de La Fontaine
> *Fables,* bk. 1 [1668], fable 8

To succeed in the world, we do
    everything we can to appear
    successful.

> François, Duc de La Rochefoucauld
> *Reflections; or, Sentences and Moral*
> *Maxims* [1678], maxim 56

The wave of the future is coming
and there is no fighting it.

> Anne Morrow Lindbergh
> *The Wave of the Future* [1940]

The appearance of a single great
genius is more than equivalent to
the birth of a hundred mediocri-
ties.

> Cesare Lombroso
> *The Man of Genius* [1891], pt. II, ch. 2

And I honor the man who is willing
to sink
Half his present repute for the freedom to think,
And, when he has thought, be his
cause strong or weak,
Will risk t' other half for the freedom
to speak.

> James Russell Lowell
> *A Fable for Critics* [1848]

In creating, the only hard thing's to
begin;
A grass-blade's no easier to make
than an oak.

> Lowell
> Ibid.

Nature fits all her children with
    something to do,
He who would write and can't write,
    can surely review.

> Lowell
> Ibid.

There is nothing more difficult to
    take in hand, more perilous to
    conduct, or more uncertain in its
    success, than to take the lead in
    the introduction of a new order of
    things.

> Niccolò Machiavelli
> *The Prince* [1532], ch. 6

Genius does what it must, and tal-
    ent does what it can.

> Edward Bulwer-Lytton,
>   Earl of Lytton [Owen Meredith]
> "Last Words of a Sensitive Second-
>   Rate Poet"

The creed which accepts as the
    foundation of morals Utility, or
    the Greatest Happiness Princi-
    ple, holds that actions are right in
    proportion as they tend to pro-
    mote happiness, wrong as they
    tend to produce the reverse of
    happiness.

> John Stuart Mill
> *Utilitarianism* [1863], ch. 2

There is no such thing as absolute certainty, but there is assurance sufficient for the purposes of human life.

Mill
On Liberty [1859], ch. 2

My trade and my art is living.

Michel de Montaigne
Essays [1580], bk. II, ch. 6

If everyone were clothed with integrity, if every heart were just, frank, kindly, the other virtues would be well-nigh useless, since their chief purpose is to make us bear with patience the injustice of our fellows.

Molière
Le Misanthrope [1666], act V, sc. i

I continue to work with the materials I have, the materials I am made of. With feelings, beings, books, events, and battles, I am omnivorous. I would like to swallow the whole earth. I would like to drink the whole sea.

Pablo Neruda
*Confieso Que He Vivido: Memorias
(Memoirs)* [1974], ch. 11

To set the cause above renown,
To love the game beyond the prize,
To honor, while you strike him down,
The foe that comes with fearless
    eyes;
To count the life of battle good
And dear the land that gave you birth,
And dearer yet the brotherhood
That binds the brave of all the earth.

> Sir Henry Newbolt
> *The Island Race*. Clifton Chapel, st. 2

Nothing worth doing is completed
in our lifetime; therefore, we
must be saved by hope. Nothing
true or beautiful or good makes
complete sense in any immediate
context of history; therefore, we
must be saved by faith. Nothing
we do, however virtuous, can be
accomplished alone; therefore,
we are saved by love.

> Reinhold Niebuhr
> *The Irony of American History* [1952]

One does not know — cannot
know — the best that is in one.

> Friedrich Nietzsche
> *Beyond Good and Evil* [1885–1886],
> IV, 240

We are the music-makers,
And we are the dreamers of dreams,
Wandering by lone sea breakers,
And sitting by desolate streams;
World-losers and world-forsakers,
On whom the pale moon gleams:
Yet we are the movers and shakers
Of the world forever, it seems.

> Arthur O'Shaughnessy
> Ode, st. 1

And now I have finished a work that neither the wrath of love, nor fire, nor the sword, nor devouring age shall be able to destroy.

> Ovid
> *Metamorphoses*, XV, 871

I wanted to use what I was, to be what I was born to be — not to have a "career," but to be that straightforward obvious unmistakable animal, a writer.

> Cynthia Ozick
> *Metaphor and Memory* [1989]

Every experiment is like a weapon which must be used in its particular way — a spear to thrust, a club to strike. Experimenting requires a man who knows when to thrust and when to strike, each according to need and fashion.

> Philippus Aureolus Paracelsus
> *Surgeon's Book* (*Chirurgische Bucher*) [1605]

No physician, insofar as he is a physician, considers his own good in what he prescribes, but the good of his patient; for the true physician is also a ruler having the human body as a subject, and is not a mere moneymaker.

> Plato
> *The Republic*, bk. I, 342–D

Genius . . . is the capacity to see ten things where the ordinary man sees one, and where the man of talent sees two or three, *plus* the ability to register that multiple perception in the material of his art.

> Ezra Pound
> *Jefferson and/or Mussolini* [1935]

The idea does not belong to the soul; it is the soul that belongs to the idea.

> Charles Sanders Peirce
> *Collected Papers* [1931–1958],
> vol. I, par. 216

They who dream by day are cognizant of many things which escape those who dream only by night.

> Edgar Allan Poe
> "Eleonora" [1841]

Immortality is to labor at an eternal task.

> Ernest Renan
> *L'Avenir de la science* [1890], preface

Nothing great is achieved without chimeras.

> Renan
> Ibid. ch. 19

I have entered on an enterprise which is without precedent, and will have no imitator. I propose to show my fellows a man as nature made him, and this man shall be myself.

> Jean Jacques Rousseau
> *Confessions* [1781–1788], I

He is the greatest artist who has embodied, in the sum of his works, the greatest number of the greatest ideas.

> Ruskin
> *Modern Painters,* vol. I [1843],
> pt. I, ch. 2

When the One Great Scorer comes to write against your name —
He marks — not that you won or lost — but how you played the game.

> Grantland Rice
> "Alumnus Football"

All great art is the work of the whole living creature, body and soul, and chiefly of the soul.

> John Ruskin
> *The Stones of Venice* [1851–1853],
> vol. I, ch. 4

Posterity weaves no garlands for
imitators.

>Friedrich von Schiller
>*Wallenstein's Camp* [1798], prologue

The will to do, the soul to dare.

>Sir Walter Scott
>*The Lady of the Lake* [1810],
>canto I, st. 21

Never have I thought that I was the
happy possessor of a "talent"; my
sole concern has been to save
myself by work and faith.

>Jean Paul Sartre
>*Les Mots* (*The Words*) [1964]

Entrepreneurial profit . . . is the
expression of the value of what
the entrepreneur contributes to
production in exactly the same
sense that wages are the value
expression of what the worker
"produces." It is not a profit of
exploitation any more than are
wages.

>Joseph Alois Schumpeter
>*The Theory of Economic Development*
>[1934], ch. 4

A lawyer without history or literature is a mechanic, a mere working mason; if he possesses some
knowledge of these, he may ven-
ture to call himself an architect.

>Scott
>*Guy Mannering* [1815], ch. 37

All art is but imitation of nature.

> Seneca
> *Epistles,* 65, 3

Be not afraid of greatness: some are born great, some achieve greatness, and some have greatness thrust upon them.

> William Shakespeare
> *Twelfth-Night* act II, sc. v, l. 159

[The law] is a jealous mistress, and requires a long and constant courtship. It is not to be won by trifling favors, but by lavish homage.

> Joseph Story
> "The Value and Importance of Legal Studies" [August 5, 1829]

Every man loves what he is good at.

> Thomas Shadwell
> *A True Widow* [1679], act V, sc. i

Perpetual devotion to what a man calls his business, is only to be sustained by perpetual neglect of many other things.

> Robert Louis Stevenson
> *Virginibus Puerisque* [1881], I. An Apology for Idlers

Discovery consists of seeing what everybody has seen and thinking what nobody has thought.

> Albert Szent-Györgyi von Nagyrapolt
> From I. J. Good (ed.), *The Scientist Speculates* [1962]

The real scientist . . . is ready to bear privation and, if need be, starvation rather than let anyone dictate to him which direction his work must take.

>Szent-Györgyi
>Science Needs Freedom. From *World Digest* [1943]

So many worlds, so much to do,
So little done, such things to be.

>Alfred, Lord Tennyson
>*In Memoriam* [1850], 73, st. 1

As for doing good, that is one of the professions which are full.

>Henry David Thoreau
>*Walden* [1854]. 1, Economy

I came into this world, not chiefly to make this a good place to live in, but to live in it, be it good or bad.

>Thoreau
>*Civil Disobedience* [1849]

He had talents equal to business, and aspired no higher.

>Tacitus
>*Annals,* bk. VI, 39

Out of the frying pan into the fire.

>Tertullian
>*De Carne Christi,* 6

Beware of all enterprises that require new clothes.

>Thoreau
>Ibid.

I share no man's opinions; I have my own.

> Ivan Turgenev
> *Fathers and Sons* [1862], ch. 13

The things we know best are those we have not learned.

> Luc de Clapiers, Marquis de
> Vauvenargues
> *Réflexions et Maximes* [c. 1747],
> no. 479

I know of no more encouraging fact than the unquestionable ability of man to elevate his life by a conscious endeavor.

> Thoreau
> *Walden.* 2, Where I Lived, and What I
> Lived For

Every peasant has a lawyer inside of him, just as every lawyer, no matter how urbane he may be, carries a peasant within himself.

> Miguel de Unamuno
> *Civilization Is Civilism*

In the future everyone will be world-famous for fifteen minutes.

> Andy Warhol
> Catalogue of his photo exhibition in
> Stockholm [1968]

No man but feels more of a man in the world if he have a bit of ground that he can call his own. However small it is on the surface, it is four thousand miles deep; and that is a very handsome property.

> Charles Dudley Warner
> *My Summer in a Garden* [1870].
> Preliminary

Justice, sir, is the great interest of man on earth.

> Daniel Webster
> On Mr. Justice Story [September 12, 1845]

To own a bit of ground, to scratch it with a hoe, to plant seeds, and watch the renewal of life — this is the commonest delight of the race, the most satisfactory thing a man can do.

> Warner
> Ibid.

Men hang out their signs indicative of their respective trades: shoe-makers hang out a gigantic shoe; jewelers, a monster watch; and the dentist hangs out a gold tooth; but up in the mountains of New Hampshire, God Almighty has hung out a sign to show that there He makes men.

> Webster
> On the Old Man of the Mountain, attributed

Publish and be damned.

> Arthur Wellesley, Duke of Wellington
> Attributed; when courtesan Harriette
> Wilson threatened to publish her
> memoirs and his letters

Inspiration descends only in flashes,
to clothe circumstances; it is not
stored up in a barrel, like salt her-
rings, to be doled out.

> Patrick White
> *Voss* [1957], ch. 2

The vitality of thought is in adventure. *Ideas won't keep.* Something
must be done about them. When
the idea is new, its custodians
have fervor, live for it, and, if
need be, die for it.

> Alfred North Whitehead
> *Dialogues of Alfred North Whitehead*
> [1953], ch. 12, April 28, 1938

I dream in my dream all the dreams
of the other dreamers,
And I become the other dreamers.

> Walt Whitman
> *Leaves of Grass* [1891–1892 ed.].
> The Sleepers, 1

The independent scientist who is worth the slightest consideration as a scientist has a consecration which comes entirely from within himself: a vocation which demands the possibility of supreme self-sacrifice.

> Norbert Wiener
> *The Human Use of Human Beings*
> [1950]

For to articulate sweet sounds together
Is to work harder than all these, and yet
Be thought an idler by the noisy set
Of bankers, schoolmasters, and clergymen
The martyrs call the world.

> William Butler Yeats
> *In the Seven Woods* [1904].
> Adam's Curse, st. I

In dreams begins responsibility.

> Yeats
> *Responsibilities* [1914], epigraph (from an old play)

At thirty, a man suspects himself a
fool;
Knows it at forty, and reforms his
plan;
At fifty chides his infamous delay,
Pushes his prudent purpose to re-
solve;
In all the magnanimity of thought
Resolves, and re-resolves; then dies
the same.

Edward Young
Night Thoughts [1742–1745].
Night I, 1. 417

A work of art is a corner of creation
seen through a temperament.

Emile Zola
My Hates [1866]

My own art is a negation of society,
an affirmation of the individual,
outside all rules and demands of
society.

Zola
Ibid.

Management

Power tends to corrupt and absolute power corrupts absolutely.

>   John Dalberg-Acton, Lord Acton
>   Letter to Bishop Mandell Creighton
>   [April 5, 1887]

Christmas is over and Business is
Business.

>   F. P. Adams
>   "For the Other 364 Days"

Never give a sucker an even break.

>   Edward Francis Albee
>   Remark

Up, to the office . . . and so to bed.

>   Franklin Pierce Adams
>   "A Ballade of Mr. Samuel Pepys."
>   Refrain

Power when wielded by abnormal
energy is the most serious of
facts.

>   Henry Adams
>   *The Education of Henry Adams* [1907],
>   ch. 28

The true teacher defends his pupils
against his own personal influence. He inspires self-trust. He
guides their eyes from himself to
the spirit that quickens him. He
will have no disciple.

>   Bronson Alcott
>   Orphic Sayings. From *The Dial*
>   [July 1840]. The Teacher

What Price Glory?

> Maxwell Anderson and Laurence
> Stallings
> Title of play [1924]

Winning isn't everything, it's the
only thing.

> Anonymous
> Saying [1953], often attributed to foot-
> ball coach Red Sanders

Give what you command, and
command what you will.

> Saint Augustine
> *Confessions* [397–401], X, 29

After this time I surpassed all others in authority, but I had no
more power than the others who
were also my colleagues in office.

> Augustus Caesar
> *Res Gestae*, 34

Before you trust a man, eat a peck
of salt with him.

> Anonymous proverb

They should rule who are able to
rule best.

> Aristotle
> *Politics,* bk. II, ch. 11

Hear the other side.

> Saint Augustine
> *De Duabus Animabus*, XIV, 2

Cure the disease and kill the patient.

> Francis Bacon
> *Essays* [1625]. Of Friendship

There's a sucker born every minute.

Phineas T. Barnum
Attributed

Judging by the virtues expected of a servant, does your Excellency know many masters who would be worthy valets?

Pierre de Beaumarchais
Le Barbier de Séville [1775], act I, sc. ii

The moment a woman gets power, she loses the solidarity she had with other women. She will want to be equal in a man's world and will become ambitious for her own sake.

Simone de Beauvoir
Interview [1984]

Call no man foe, but never love a stranger.

Stella Benson
"To the Unborn," st. 3

Nothing happens, nobody comes, nobody goes, it's awful!

Samuel Beckett
Waiting for Godot [1952], act I

Intelligence . . . is the faculty of making artificial objects, especially tools to make tools.

Henri Bergson
L'Evolution créatrice (*Creative Evolution*) [1907], ch. 2

Be swift to hear, slow to speak, slow
   to wrath:
For the wrath of man worketh not the
   righteousness of God.

> The Bible
> New Testament
> James 1:19–20

Come unto me, all ye that labor and
   are heavy laden, and I will give
   you rest.
   Take my yoke upon you, and
   learn of me; for I am meek and
   lowly in heart: and ye shall find
   rest unto your souls.
   For my yoke is easy, and my
   burden is light.

> New Testament
> Matthew 11:28–30

For unto whomsoever much is
   given, of him shall be much required: and to whom men have
   committed much, of him they
   will ask the more.

> New Testament
> Luke 12:48

He that is not with me is against
   me.

> New Testament
> Matthew 12:30

The law is good, if a man use it lawfully.

> New Testament
> I Timothy 1:8

The tree is known by his fruit.

> New Testament
> Matthew 12:33

He that is today a king tomorrow shall die.

> Apocrypha
> The Wisdom of Jesus the Son of Sirach, or Ecclesiasticus 10:10

Many are in high place, and of renown: but mysteries are revealed unto the meek.

> Apocrypha
> The Wisdom of Jesus the Son of Sirach, or Ecclesiasticus 3:19

Multitudes in the valley of decision.

> Old Testament
> Joel 3:14

The greater thou art, the more humble thyself.

> Apocrypha
> The Wisdom of Jesus the Son of Sirach, or Ecclesiasticus 3:18

The most potent weapon in the hands of the oppressor is the mind of the oppressed.

> Steve Biko
> Statement as witness [May 3, 1976]

An example from the monkey: The higher it climbs, the more you see of its behind.

> Saint Bonaventure
> Conferences on the Gospel of John

If we would guide by the light of reason, we must let our minds be bold.

> Louis D. Brandeis
> *New State Ice Co.* v. *Liebmann,* 285 U.S. 262,311 [1932]

The right people in the right jobs.

> Otto von Bismarck
> Speech to the North German Reichstag [1875]

Authority without wisdom is like a heavy axe without an edge, fitter to bruise than polish.

> Anne Bradstreet
> *Meditations Divine and Moral* [1664], 12

Grub first: then ethics.

> Bertolt Brecht
> *The Threepenny Opera* [1928], act II, sc. i

I gave commands;
Then all smiles stopped together.

> Robert Browning
> "My Last Duchess" [1842], l. 45

He that wrestles with us strengthens our nerves, and sharpens our skill. Our antagonist is our helper.

> Edmund Burke
> *Reflections on the Revolution in France* [1790]

A hen is only an egg's way of making another egg.

> Samuel Butler
> *Life and Habit* [1877], ch. 8

What has once been settled by a precedent will not be unsettled overnight, for certainty and uniformity are gains not lightly to be sacrificed.

> Benjamin Cardozo
> *The Paradoxes of Legal Science* [1928]

"A fair day's wages for a fair day's work": it is as just a demand as governed men ever made of governing. It is the everlasting right of man.

> Thomas Carlyle
> *Past and Present* [1843], bk. I, ch. 3

Democracy is, by the nature of it, a self-canceling business; and gives in the long run a net result of zero.

> Carlyle
> *Chartism* [1839], ch. 6, Laissez-Faire

"If everybody minded their own business," said the Duchess in a hoarse growl, "the world would go round a deal faster than it does."

> Lewis Carroll
> *Alice's Adventures in Wonderland*
> [1865], ch. 6

Captains of Industry.

> Carlyle
> Ibid. bk. IV, ch. 4 (chapter title)

Those who would administer wisely must, indeed, be wise, for one of the serious obstacles to the improvement of our race is indiscriminate charity.

> Andrew Carnegie
> Wealth. From the *North American Review* [June 1889]

The first step in providing economic equality for women is to ensure a stable economy in which every person who wants to work can work.

> Jimmy Carter
> Speech at Women's Agenda Conference, Washington, D.C.
> [October 2, 1976]

No one can build his security upon
the nobleness of another person.

> Willa Cather
> *Alexander's Bridge* [1912], ch. 8

A finger in every pie.

> Miguel de Cervantes
> *Don Quixote de la Mancha,* pt. I
> [1605], bk. III, ch. 6

The maxim of the British people is
"Business as usual."

> Winston Churchill
> Speech at the Guildhall
> [November 9, 1914]

Wise men profit more from fools
than fools from wise men; for the
wise men shun the mistakes of
fools, but fools do not imitate the
successes of the wise.

> Cato the Elder
> From Plutarch, *Lives,* Cato, sec. 9

We prove what we want to prove,
and the real difficulty is to know
what we want to prove.

> Émile Auguste Chartier [Alain]
> *Système des beaux-arts* [1920]

If a man aspires to the highest place, it is no dishonor to him to halt at the second, or even at the third.

> Cicero
> *Orator,* 4

By God, Mr. Chairman, at this moment I stand astonished at my own moderation!

> Robert, Lord Clive
> Reply during Parliamentary Inquiry
> [1773]

[The superior man] acts before he speaks, and afterwards speaks according to his actions.

> Confucius
> *The Confucian Analects,* bk. 2:13

Good government obtains when those who are near are made happy, and those who are far off are attracted.

> Confucius
> Ibid. bk. 13:16, ii

The people may be made to follow a path of action, but they may not be made to understand it.

> Confucius
> Ibid. bk. 8:9

All ambitions are lawful except
those which climb upward on the
miseries or credulities of mankind.

> Joseph Conrad
> *A Personal Record* [1912], preface

The chief business of the American
people is business.

> Calvin Coolidge
> Speech to the American Society of
> Newspaper Editors [January 17,
> 1925]

To conquer without risk is to
triumph without glory.

> Pierre Corneille
> *Le Cid* [1636], act II, sc. ii

Let a fool be made serviceable according to his folly.

> Conrad
> *Under Western Eyes* [1911], pt. I, ch. 3

When a great many people are un-
able to find work, unemployment
results.

> Coolidge
> Attributed

Who is all-powerful should fear
everything.

> Corneille
> *Cinna* [1640], act IV, sc. ii

A fair request should be followed by
the deed in silence.

> Dante
> *The Divine Comedy* [c. 1310–1321].
> Inferno, canto XXIV, l. 77

Worldly renown is naught but a
breath of wind, which now comes
this way and now comes that, and
changes name because it changes
quarter.

> Dante
> Ibid. Purgatorio, canto XI, l. 100

"Do other men for they would do
you." That's the true business
precept.

> Charles Dickens
> *Martin Chuzzlewit* [1843–1844], ch. 11

Take nothing on its looks; take everything on evidence. There's no
better rule.

> Dickens
> *Great Expectations* [1860–1861],
> ch. 40

We must scrunch or be scrunched.

> Dickens
> *Our Mutual Friend* [1864–1865],
> bk. III, ch. 5

Whatever was required to be done, the Circumlocution Office was beforehand with all the public departments in the art of perceiving — HOW NOT TO DO IT.

> Dickens
> *Little Dorrit* [1857–1858], bk. I, ch. 10

How much easier it is to be critical than to be correct.

> Benjamin Disraeli
> Speech [January 24, 1860]

I have climbed to the top of the greasy pole.

> Disraeli
> To friends, on being made prime
> minister [1868]

I repeat . . . that all power is a trust; that we are accountable for its exercise; that, from the people, and for the people, all springs, and all must exist.

> Disraeli
> *Vivian Grey* [1826], bk. VI, ch. 7

What we anticipate seldom occurs; what we least expected generally happens.

> Disraeli
> *Henrietta Temple* [1837], bk. II, ch. 4

When a man fell into his anecdotage, it was a sign for him to retire.

> Disraeli
> *Lothair* [1870], ch. 28

You have seen how a man was made a slave; you shall see how a slave was made a man.

> Douglass
> *Narrative of the Life of Frederick Douglass* [1845], ch. 10

Nice Guys Finish Last.

> Leo Durocher
> Title of book [1975]

No man can put a chain about the ankle of his fellow man without at last finding the other end fastened about his own neck.

> Frederick Douglass
> Speech at Civil Rights Mass Meeting, Washington, D.C. [October 22, 1883]

You will be damned if you do — And you will be damned if you don't [definition of Calvinism].

> Lorenzo Dow
> *Reflections on the Love of God*

The more wise and powerful a master, the more directly is his work created, and the simpler it is.

> Meister Eckhart
> *Of the Eternal Birth*

A patronizing disposition always has
its meaner side.

George Eliot
Adam Bede [1859], ch. 27

He was like a cock who thought the
sun had risen to hear him crow.

George Eliot
Ibid. ch. 33

'Tis God gives skill,
But not without men's hands: He
could not make
Antonio Stradivari's violins
Without Antonio.

George Eliot
"Stradivarius"

We fight for lost causes because we
know that our defeat and dismay
may be the preface to our succes-
sors' victory, though that victory
itself will be temporary; we fight
rather to keep something alive
than in the expectation that anything will triumph.

T. S. Eliot
For Lancelot Andrews [1928]. Francis
Herbert Bradley

Most editors are failed writers —
but so are most writers.

T. S. Eliot
From Robert Giroux, *The Education of
An Editor* [1982]

Not fare well,
But fare forward, voyagers.

> T. S. Eliot
> *Four Quartets.* The Dry Salvages
> [1941], III

The greatest task before civilization
at present is to make machines
what they ought to be, the slaves,
instead of the masters of men.

> Havelock Ellis
> *Little Essays of Love and Virtue* [1922],
> ch. 7

To be a leader of men one must
turn one's back on men.

> Ellis
> Introduction to Joris-Karl Huysmans,
> *À Rebours* (*Against the Grain*) [1884]

An institution is the lengthened
shadow of one man.

> Ralph Waldo Emerson
> *Essays: First Series* [1841]. Self-
> Reliance

If the single man plant himself in-
domitably on his instincts, and
there abide, the huge world will
come round to him.

> Emerson
> *The American Scholar* [1837], sec. 3

Nothing astonishes men so much as common sense and plain dealing.

> Emerson
> *Essays: First Series.* Art

To be great is to be misunderstood.

> Emerson
> Ibid. Self-Reliance

You shall have joy, or you shall have power, said God; you shall not have both.

> Emerson
> *Journal.* October 1842

Remember that you ought to behave in life as you would at a banquet. As something is being passed around it comes to you; stretch out your hand, take a portion of it politely. It passes on; do not detain it. Or it has not come to you yet; do not project your desire to meet it, but wait until it comes in front of you. So act toward children, so toward a wife, so toward office, so toward wealth.

> Epictetus
> *The Encheiridion,* 15

Each year new consuls and proconsuls are made; but not every year is a king or a poet born.

> Lucius Annaeus Florus
> *De Qualitate Vitae,* fragment 8

The whole art of teaching is only the art of awakening the natural curiosity of young minds for the purpose of satisfying it afterwards.

> Anatole France
> *The Crime of Sylvestre Bonnard* [1881], pt. II, ch. 4

The world cannot live at the level of its great men.

> Sir James Frazer
> *The Golden Bough* [1922], ch. 37

Synergy means behavior of whole systems unpredicted by the behavior of their parts.

> R. Buckminster Fuller
> *What I Have Learned* [1966]. How Little I Know

Much of the world's work, it has been said, is done by men who do not feel quite well. [Karl] Marx is a case in point.

> John Kenneth Galbraith
> *The Age of Uncertainty* [1977], ch. 3

The leisure class has been replaced
by another and much larger class
to which work has none of the
older connotation of pain, fatigue,
or other mental or physical dis-
comfort. We have failed to observe the emergence of this New
Class, as it may be simply called.

Galbraith
The Affluent Society [1958], ch. 24

At five in the afternoon.
Ah, that fatal five in the afternoon!
It was five by all the clocks!
It was five in the shade of the after-
noon!

Federico García Lorca
Lament for Ignacio Sanchez Mejias
(*Llanto por Ignacio Sanchez Mejias*)
[1935], I

With reasonable men, I will reason;
with humane men I will plead;
but to tyrants I will give no quarter, nor waste arguments where
they will certainly be lost.

William Lloyd Garrison
W. P. and F. J. T. Garrison, *William
Lloyd Garrison* [1885–1889],
vol. I, p. 188

I hate the man who builds his name
On ruins of another's fame.

> John Gay
> *Fables*, pt. I [1727]. The Poet and the
>   Rose

In every age and clime we see
Two of a trade can never agree.

> Gay
> Ibid. The Rat-catcher and Cats

I am the Captain of the *Pinafore*;
And a right good captain too!

> Sir William S. Gilbert
> *H.M.S. Pinafore* [1878], act I

It is, it is a glorious thing
To be a Pirate King.

> Gilbert
> *Pirates of Penzance* [1879], act I

Stick close to your desks and *never
   go to sea,*
And you all may be Rulers of the
   Queen's Navee!

> Gilbert
> *H.M.S. Pinafore* [1878], act I

The Law is the true embodiment
Of everything that's excellent.
It has no kind of fault or flaw,
And I, my Lords, embody the Law.

> Gilbert
> *Iolanthe* [1882], act I

When everyone is somebodee,
Then no one's anybody!

>Gilbert
>*The Gondoliers* [1889], act II

There's a whining at the thresh-
old —
There's a scratching at the floor —
To work! To work! In Heaven's name!
The wolf is at the door!

>Charlotte Perkins Gilman
>*In This Our World* [1893]. The Wolf at
>the Door, st. 6

Decision by majorities is as much
an expedient as lighting by gas.

>William Gladstone
>Speech in the House of Commons
>[1858]

The deed is everything, the glory
nothing.

>Johann Wolfgang von Goethe
>*Faust*. The Second Part [1832], act IV,
>A High Mountain Range

A verbal agreement isn't worth the
paper it's written on.

>Samuel Goldwyn
>Attributed

Our worst enemies here are not the ignorant and the simple, however cruel; our worst enemies are the intelligent and corrupt.

> Graham Greene
> *The Human Factor* [1978], pt. III, ch. 3

Mark this well, you proud men of action: You are nothing but the unwitting agents of the men of thought who often, in quiet self-effacement, mark out most exactly all your doings in advance.

> Heinrich Heine
> *History of Religion and Philosophy in Germany* [1834], vol. III

People in those old times had convictions; we moderns only have opinions. And it needs more than a mere opinion to erect a Gothic cathedral.

> Heine
> *The French Stage* [1837], ch. 9

Force has no place where there is need of skill.

> Herodotus
> *The Histories of Herodotus,*
> bk. III, ch. 127.

It is better to be envied than pitied.

>Herodotus
>Ibid. bk. III, ch. 52

Hold their noses to grindstone.

>Heywood
>Ibid. ch. 5.

A majority can never replace the man. . . . Just as a hundred fools do not make one wise man, an heroic decision is not likely to come from a hundred cowards.

>Adolf Hitler
>*Mein Kampf* (*My Battle*) [1933], vol. I, ch. 3

Haste in every business brings failures.

>Herodotus
>Ibid. bk. VII, ch. 10

A man may well bring a horse to the water,
But he cannot make him drink without he will.

>John Heywood
>*Proverbs* [1547], pt. I, ch. 11

Rome was not built in one day.

>Heywood
>Ibid. ch. 11

A great man represents a great ganglion in the nerves of society, or, to vary the figure, a strategic point in the campaign of history, and part of his greatness consists in his being *there*.

> Oliver Wendell Holmes, Jr.
> *John Marshall* [1901]

The only prize much cared for by the powerful is power. The prize of the general is not a bigger tent, but command.

> Holmes
> *Law and the Court* [1913]

Strength lies not in defense but in attack.

> Hitler
> Ibid.

I dare say that I have worked off my fundamental formula on you that the chief end of man is to frame general propositions and that no general proposition is worth a damn.

> Holmes
> Letter to Sir Frederick Pollock [1920]

Young man, the secret of my success is that at an early age I discovered I was not God.

> Holmes
> Reply to a reporter's question on his ninetieth birthday [March 8, 1931]

A multitude of rulers is not a good
thing. Let there be one ruler, one
king.

> Homer
> *The Iliad*, bk. II, l. 204

Of men who have a sense of honor,
more come through alive than are
slain, but from those who flee
comes neither glory nor any help.

> Homer
> Ibid. bk. XV, l. 563

You will certainly not be able to
take the lead in all things yourself, for to one man a god has
given deeds of war, and to another the dance, to another the
lyre and song, and in another
wide-sounding Zeus puts a good
mind.

> Homer
> Ibid. bk. XIII, l. 729

Young men's minds are always
changeable, but when an old man
is concerned in a matter, he looks
both before and after.

> Homer
> Ibid. bk. III, l. 108

If capital an' labor ever do git
t'gether it's good night fer th' rest
of us.

> Frank Hubbard [Abe Martin]
> Saying

When you send a clerk on business to a distant province, a man of rigid morals is not your best choice.

> Ihara Saikaku
> *The Japanese Family Storehouse; or, The Millionaires' Gospel*, bk. II, ch. 5

The art of being wise is the art of knowing what to overlook.

> William James
> *The Principles of Psychology* [1890], ch. 22

The minority is always right.

> Henrik Ibsen
> *An Enemy of the People* [1882], act IV

To criticize is to appreciate, to appropriate, to take intellectual possession, to establish in fine a relation with the criticized thing and to make it one's own.

> Henry James
> *Prefaces* [1907–1909]. *What Maisie Knew*

Merchants have no country. The mere spot they stand on does not constitute so strong an attachment as that from which they draw their gains.

> Thomas Jefferson
> Letter to Horatio G. Spafford [March 17, 1814]

An unstable pilot steers a leaking
ship, and the blind is leading the
blind straight to the pit. The ruler
is like the ruled.

> Saint Jerome
> Letter 7

This nation, this generation, in this
hour has man's first chance to
build a Great Society, a place
where the meaning of man's life
matches the marvels of man's
labor.

> Lyndon B. Johnson
> Address, accepting the presidential
> nomination [August 1964]

Every race and every nation should
be judged by the best it has been
able to produce, not by the worst.

> James Weldon Johnson
> *The Autobiography of an Ex-Colored
> Man* [1912], ch. 10

The more things change, the more
they remain the same.

> Alphonse Karr
> *Les Guêpes* [January 1849]

When you can measure what you are speaking about, and express it in numbers, you know something about it; but when you cannot measure it, when you cannot express it in numbers, your knowledge is of a meager and unsatisfactory kind: it may be the beginning of knowledge, but you have scarcely, in your thoughts, advanced to the stage of *science*.

> William Thomson, Lord Kelvin
> *Popular Lectures and Addresses*
> [1891–1894]

Power is the great aphrodisiac.

> Henry A. Kissinger
> In the *New York Times*
> [January 19, 1971]

More men are killed by overwork than the importance of the world justifies.

> Rudyard Kipling
> *The Phantom 'Rickshaw* [1888]

Market competition is the only form of organization which can afford a large measure of freedom to the individual.

> Frank Hyneman Knight
> *Freedom and Reform* [1947], ch. 13

The only reason people want to be masters of the future is to change the past.

> Milan Kundera
> *The Book of Laughter and Forgetting* [1980], pt. I, sec. xvii

The opinion of the strongest is always the best.

> La Fontaine
> Ibid. bk. I [1668], fable 10

People are difficult to govern because they have too much knowledge.

> Lao-tzu
> *The Way of Lao-tzu*, 65

If we had no faults of our own, we would not take so much pleasure in noticing those of others.

> François, Duc de La Rochefoucauld
> *Reflections; or, Sentences and Moral Maxims* [1678], maxim 31

Beware, as long as you live, of judging people by appearances.

> Jean de La Fontaine
> *Fables*, bk. VI [1668], fable 5

The sign brings customers.

> La Fontaine
> Ibid. bk. VII [1678–1679], fable l5

The more laws and order are made prominent,
The more thieves and robbers there will be.

> Lao-tzu
> Ibid. 57

It would be madness to let the purposes or the methods of private enterprise set the habits of the age of atomic energy.

> Harold J. Laski
> *Plan or Perish* [1945]

No snowflake in an avalanche ever feels responsible.

> Stanislaw Jerzy Lec
> *More Unkempt Thoughts* [1968]

Important principles may and must be inflexible.

> Abraham Lincoln
> Last public address, Washington, D.C.
> [April 11, 1865]

We always like those who admire us; we do not always like those whom we admire.

> La Rochefoucauld
> Ibid. maxim 294

There could be no honor in a sure success, but much might be wrested from a sure defeat.

> T. E. Lawrence
> *Revolt in the Desert* [1927], ch. 19

Whoever in discussion adduces authority uses not intellect but rather memory.

> Leonardo da Vinci
> *The Notebooks*, vol. 1, ch. 2

Let us have faith that right makes might, and in that faith let us to the end dare to do our duty as we understand it.

Lincoln
Address at Cooper Union, New York
[February 27, 1860]

The final test of a leader is that he leaves behind him in other men the conviction and the will to carry on. . . . The genius of a good leader is to leave behind him a situation which common sense, without the grace of genius, can deal with successfully.

Walter Lippmann
"Roosevelt Has Gone" [April 14, 1945]

It may seem strange that any men should dare to ask a just God's assistance in wringing their bread from the sweat of other men's faces, but let us judge not, that we be not judged.

Lincoln
Second Inaugural Address
[March 4, 1865]

A professor can never better distinguish himself in his work than by encouraging a clever pupil, for the true discoverers are among them, as comets amongst the stars.

Linnaeus
From a biography of Linnaeus by
Benjamin Daydon Jones, ch. 9

Monopoly is Business at the end of
its journey.

> Lloyd
> Ibid.

New opinions are always suspected,
and usually opposed, without any
other reason but because they are
not already common.

> Locke
> Ibid. Dedicatory epistle

Things always seem fairer when we
look back at them, and it is out of
that inaccessible tower of the
past that Longing leans and beck-
ons.

> Lowell
> *Literary Essays,* vol. I [1864–1890].
> A Few Bits of Roman Mosaic

Corporations have no souls, but
they can love each other.

> Henry Demarest Lloyd
> *Wealth Against Commonwealth* [1894]

It is one thing to show a man that
he is in an error, and another to
put him in possession of truth.

> John Locke
> *Essay Concerning Human Understand-
> ing* [1690], bk. IV, ch. 7, sec. 11

It is by presence of mind in untried
emergencies that the native metal
of a man is tested.

> James Russell Lowell
> "Abraham Lincoln" [1864]

Soon fades the spell, soon comes
   the night;
Say will it not be then the same,
Whether we played the black or
   white,
Whether we lost or won the game?

> Thomas Babington, Lord Macaulay
> "Sermon in a Churchyard," st. 8

When I find the road narrow, and
   can see no other way of teaching
   a well-established truth except by
   pleasing one intelligent man and
   displeasing ten thousand
   fools — I prefer to address myself
   to the one man.

> Maimonides
> *The Guide for the Perplexed* [1190].
> Introduction

Success is like some horrible disaster
Worse than your house burning.

> Malcolm Lowry
> After publication of *Under the Volcano*
> [1962]

Men are never so likely to settle a
   question rightly as when they
   discuss it freely.

> Lord Macaulay
> *Southey's Colloquies on Society* [1830]

Opinions cannot survive if one has
   no chance to fight for them.

> Thomas Mann
> *The Magic Mountain* [1924], ch. 6

We are most likely to get angry and excited in our opposition to some idea when we ourselves are not quite certain of our own position, and are inwardly tempted to take the other side.

> Mann
> *Buddenbrooks* [1903], pt. VIII, ch. 2

What is not good for the swarm is not good for the bee.

> Marcus Aurelius
> Ibid. VI, 54

All is ephemeral — fame and the famous as well.

> Marcus Aurelius
> *Meditations*, IV, 35

an optimist is a guy
that has never had
much experience

> Don Marquis
> *archy and mehitabel* [1927]. certain
> maxims of archy

there is always
a comforting thought
in time of trouble when
it is not our trouble

> Marquis
> *archy does his part* [1935]. comforting
> thoughts

It is not enough to fight. It is the
spirit which we bring to the fight
that decides the issue. It is mo-
rale that wins the victory.

> George C. Marshall
> Military Review [October 1948]

The philosophers have only inter-
preted the world in various ways.
The point, however, is to change
it.

> Marx
> *Theses on Feuerbach* [1888], xi

We might as reasonably dispute
whether it is the upper or the
under blade of a pair of scissors
that cuts a piece of paper, as
whether value is governed by util-
ity or cost of production.

> Alfred Marshall
> *Principles of Economics* [1890]

The intellectual desolation, artifi-
cially produced by converting
immature human beings into
mere machines.

> Karl Marx
> *Capital* [1867–1883], pt. II, ch. 10

Be wise;
Soar not too high to fall; but stoop to
rise.

> Massinger
> *Duke of Milan* [1623], act I, sc. ii

To give the throne to another man
would be easy; to find a man who
shall benefit the kingdom is difficult.

> Mencius
> *Works*, bk. III, 1:4.10

Time is a great legalizer, even in the
field of morals.

> Mencken
> *A Book of Prefaces* [1917], ch. 4

He that would govern others, first
should be
The master of himself.

> Philip Massinger
> *The Bondman* [1624], act I, sc. iii

People ask you for criticism, but
they only want praise.

> W. Somerset Maugham
> *Of Human Bondage* [1915], ch. 50

The public . . . demands certain-
ties. . . . But there *are* no certain-
ties.

> H. L. Mencken
> *Prejudices, First Series* [1919], ch. 3

When A annoys or injures B on the
pretense of saving or improving X,
A is a scoundrel.

> Mencken
> *Newspaper Days: 1899–1906* [1941]

He who knows only his own side of the case, knows little of that.

John Stuart Mill
On Liberty [1859], ch. 2

Whatever crushes individuality is despotism, by whatever name it may be called.

Mill
Ibid. ch. 3

Never fight fair with a stranger, boy. You'll never get out of the jungle that way.

Arthur Miller
Death of a Salesman [1949], act I

When I see a merchant overpolite to his customers, begging them to taste a little brandy and throwing half his goods on the counter — thinks I, that man has an ax to grind.

Charles Miner
Essays from the Desk of Poor Robert the Scribe [1815]. Who'll Turn Grindstones

Be nice to people on your way up because you'll meet them on your way down.

Wilson Mizner
Saying

The computer is no better than its program.

Elting E. Morison
Men, Machines and Modern Times
[1966]

Life always gets harder toward the summit — the cold increases, responsibility increases.

Friedrich Nietzsche
The Antichrist [1888], aphorism 57

No matter that we may mount on stilts, we still must walk on our own legs. And on the highest throne in the world, we still sit only on our own bottom.

Michel de Montaigne
Essays, bk. III [1595], ch. 13

But, in case signals can neither be seen or perfectly understood, no captain can do very wrong if he places his ship alongside that of the enemy.

Horatio Nelson
Memorandum to the fleet, off Cadiz,
October 9, 1805

Never apologize and never explain — it's a sign of weakness.

> Frank S. Nugent and Laurence Stallings
> *She Wore a Yellow Ribbon* (screenplay) [1949]

Wars may be fought with weapons, but they are won by men. It is the spirit of the men who follow and of the man who leads that gains the victory.

> George Patton
> In the *Cavalry Journal* [September 1933]

One must have a good memory to be able to keep the promises one makes.

> Nietzsche
> *Human, All Too Human* [1878], 59

Every intellectual product must be judged from the point of view of the age and the people in which it was produced.

> Walter Pater
> *Studies in the History of the Renaissance* [1873]. Mirandola

You can do anything,
But don't step on my blue suede
· shoes.

>Carl Perkins
>*Blue Suede Shoes* [1956]

Lateral Arabesque — a pseudo-
promotion consisting of a new
title and a new work place.

>Laurence J. Peter
>*The Peter Principle* [1969]

In a hierarchy, every employee
tends to rise to his level of incom-
petence.

>Peter
>Ibid.

There is something behind the
throne greater than the King himself.

>William Pitt, Earl of Chatham
>Speech in the House of Lords
> [March 2, 1770]

Unlimited power is apt to corrupt
the minds of those who possess
it; and this I know, my lords, that
where laws end, tyranny begins.

>Pitt
>Case of Wilkes. Speech
> [January 9, 1770]

In the early days of his power, he is full of smiles, and he salutes everyone whom he meets.

> Plato
> *The Republic,* bk. VIII, 566–D

The judge should not be young; he should have learned to know evil, not from his own soul, but from late and long observation of the nature of evil in others: knowledge should be his guide, not personal experience.

> Plato
> Ibid. bk. III, 409–B

When a building is about to fall down, all the mice desert it.

> Pliny the Elder
> *Natural History,* bk. VIII, 103

For to err in opinion, though it be not the part of wise men, is at least human.

> Plutarch
> *Morals.* Against Colotes

To doubt everything or to believe everything are two equally convenient solutions; both dispense with the necessity of reflection.

> Jules Henri Poincaré
> Quoted by Bertrand Russell in preface
> to *Science and Method* [1913] (*La
> Science et l'hypothèse*, 1903)

One-Upmanship.

> Potter
> Title of book [1952]

Anyone can hold the helm when the sea is calm.

> Publilius Syrus
> Maxim 358

Gamesmanship: The Art of Winning Games Without Actually Cheating.

> Stephen Potter
> Title of book [1947]

A rolling stone gathers no moss.

> Publilius Syrus
> Maxim 524

It takes a long time to bring excellence to maturity.

> Publilius Syrus
> Maxim 780

Many receive advice, few profit by it.

Publilius Syrus
Maxim 149

I'll make him an offer he can't refuse.

Mario Puzo
The Godfather [1969]

How shall I be able to rule over others, that have not full power and command of myself?

François Rabelais
Gargantua and Pantagruel, bk. I [1532], ch. 52

In a calm sea every man is a pilot.

John Ray
English Proverbs [1670]

A jackass can kick a barn down, but it takes a carpenter to build one.

Sam Rayburn
Remark [c. 1953]

Show me a good and gracious loser and I'll show you a failure.

Knute Rockne
Remark to Wisconsin basketball coach Walter Meanwell [1920s]

I joked about every prominent man
in my lifetime, but I never met
one I didn't like.

> Will Rogers
> Epitaph

Never before have we had so little
time in which to do so much.

> Franklin D. Roosevelt
> Fireside Chat [February 23, 1942]

We are moving forward to greater
freedom, to greater security for
the average man than he has ever
known before in the history of
America.

> Roosevelt
> Fireside Chat [September 30, 1934]

No one can make you feel inferior
without your consent.

> Eleanor Roosevelt
> *This Is My Story* [1937]

There is no indispensable man.

> Roosevelt
> Campaign speech, New York
> [November 3, 1932]

The lunatics have taken charge of the asylum.

Richard Rowland
Comment on the formation of United
Artists film corporation [1920]

Great souls suffer in silence.

Friedrich von Schiller
Don Carlos [1787], act I, sc. iv

The strongest is never strong enough to be always the master, unless he transforms his strength into right, and obedience into duty.

Jean Jacques Rousseau
The Social Contract [1762], I, ch. 3

Ambition drove many men to become false; to have one thought locked in the breast, another ready on the tongue.

Sallust
The War with Catiline [c. 40 B.C.], sec. 10

It is a rough road that leads to the heights of greatness.

Seneca
Epistles, 84, 13

Glory is like a circle in the water,
Which never ceaseth to enlarge itself,
Till by broad spreading it disperse to
nought.

William Shakespeare
King Henry the Sixth, Part I,
act I, sc. ii, l. 133

Spur not an unbroken horse; put not your plowshare too deep into new land.

Sir Walter Scott
The Monastery [1820]. Answer of the
Author of *Waverley* to the Letter of
Captain Clutterbuck, ch. 25

The pilot . . . who has been able to say, "Neptune, you shall never sink this ship except on an even keel," has fulfilled the require-ments of his art.

Seneca
Ibid. 85, 33

We cannot all be masters.

> Shakespeare
> *Othello*, act I, sc. i, l. 43

Good counselors lack no clients.

> Shakespeare
> *Measure for Measure*, act I, sc. ii, l. 115

He who can, does. He who cannot, teaches.

> George Bernard Shaw
> *Man and Superman* [1903]. Maxims for Revolutionists

Press not a falling man too far.

> Shakespeare
> *King Henry the Eighth*, act III, sc. ii, l. 334

We were not born to sue, but to command.

> Shakespeare
> *King John*, act I, sc. i, l. 196

'Tis mad idolatry
To make the service greater than the god.

> Shakespeare
> *Troilus and Cressida*, act II, sc. ii, l. 56

Power, like a desolating pestilence,
Pollutes whate'er it touches; and obedience,
Bane of all genius, virtue, freedom, truth,
Makes slaves of men, and, of the human frame,
A mechanized automaton.

> Percy Bysshe Shelley
> *Queen Mab* [1813], III

The real problem is not whether machines think but whether men do.

> B. F. Skinner
> *Contingencies of Reinforcement* [1969], ch. 9

People of the same trade seldom meet together, even for merriment and diversion, but the conversation ends in a conspiracy against the public, or in some contrivance to raise prices.

> Adam Smith
> *An Inquiry into the Nature and Causes of the Wealth of Nations* [1776], vol. I, bk. I, ch. 10, pt. 2.

Avoid shame, but do not seek glory — nothing so expensive as glory.

> Sydney Smith
> *Lady Holland's Memoir* [1855], vol. I, ch. 4

No one is fit to be trusted with power. . . . No one. . . . Any man who has lived at all knows the follies and wickedness he's capable of. If he does not know it, he is not fit to govern others. And if he does know it, he knows also that neither he nor any man ought to be allowed to decide a single human fate.

> C. P. Snow
> *The Light and the Dark* [1961]

How dreadful it is when the right judge judges wrong!

> Sophocles
> *Antigone* [c. 442 B.C.], l. 323

I have nothing but contempt for the kind of governor who is afraid, for whatever reason, to follow the course that he knows is best for the State; and as for the man who sets private friendship above the public welfare — I have no use for him, either.

Sophocles
Ibid. l. 181

Nobody likes the man who brings bad news.

Sophocles
Ibid. l. 277

Every cause produces more than one effect.

Herbert Spencer
Essays on Education [1861]. On Progress: Its Law and Cause

Progress, therefore, is not an accident, but a necessity. . . . It is a part of nature.

Spencer
Social Statics [1851], pt. 1, ch. 2

A dinner lubricates business.

William Scott, Lord Stowell
From James Boswell, *Life of Johnson*
[1791]

More people are flattered into virtue than bullied out of vice.

Robert Smith Surtees
The Analysis of the Hunting Field
[1846], ch. 1

We have unmistakable proof that
throughout all past time, there
has been a ceaseless devouring of
the weak by the strong.

Spencer
First Principles [1861]

Be extremely subtle, even to the
point of formlessness. Be extremely mysterious, even to the
point of soundlessness. Thereby
you can be the director of the
opponent's fate.

Sun-tzu
The Art of War. Emptiness and Full-
ness

Hail, fellow, well met,
All dirty and wet:
Find out if you can,
Who's master, who's man.

> Jonathan Swift
> "My Lady's Lamentation" [1765], l. 171

I shall be like that tree, I shall die at
the top.

> Swift
> From Sir Walter Scott, *Life of Swift*
> [1814]

Glory to Man in the highest! for
Man is the master of things.

> Algernon Charles Swinburne
> "Hymn of Man" [1871]

The desire for glory clings even to
the best men longer than any
other passion.

> Tacitus
> *Histories*, bk. IV, 6

What is today supported by prece-
dents will hereafter become a
precedent.

> Tacitus
> *Annals*, bk. XI, 24

Our little systems have their day.

> Alfred, Lord Tennyson
> *In Memoriam* [1850], Prologue, st. 5

Some sense of duty, something of
faith,
Some reverence for the laws ourselves have made,
Some patient force to change them
when we will,
Some civic manhood firm against the
crowd.

Tennyson
The Princess [1847], Conclusion, l. 54

There lives more faith in honest
doubt,
Believe me, than in half the creeds.

Tennyson
In Memoriam [1850], 96, st. 3

Perhaps it is this specter that most
haunts working men and women:
the planned obsolescence of people that is of a piece with the
planned obsolescence of the
things they make. Or sell.

Studs Terkel
Working [1972]. Introduction

One finds many companions for
food and drink, but in a serious
business a man's companions are
very few.

> Theognis
> *Elegies*, l. 115

Give a man a horse he can ride,
Give a man a boat he can sail.

> James Thomson
> "Sunday Up the River" [1869], st. 15

It is better to know some of the
questions than all of the answers.

> James Thurber
> Saying

They who are in highest places, and
have the most power, have the
least liberty, because they are
most observed.

> John Tillotson
> *Reflections*

The strongest of all warriors are
these two — Time and Patience.

> Leo Tolstoi
> *War and Peace* [1865–1869],
> bk. X, ch. 16

If you can't stand the heat, get out
of the kitchen.

> Harry S. Truman
> Saying

Once a decision was made, I did
not worry about it afterward.

> Truman
> *Memoirs* [1955], vol. II. *Years of Trial
> and Hope,* ch. 1

The buck stops here.

> Truman
> Sign on Truman's desk when President.
> From Alfred Steinberg, *The Man from
> Missouri* [1962]

He who is the ruler of men takes
non-action as his way and
considers impartiality as his
treasure. He sits upon the throne
of non-action and rides upon
the perfection of his officials.

> Tung Chung-shu
> *Ch'un-ch'iu fan-lu*

Well-timed silence hath more eloquence than speech.

> Martin Farquhar Tupper
> *Proverbial Philosophy* [1838–1842].
> Of Discretion

I propose to consider the question,
"Can machines think?"

> Alan M. Turing
> "Computing Machinery and Intelli-
> gence" [October 1950]

Training is everything. The peach was once a bitter almond; cauliflower is nothing but cabbage with a college education.

> Mark Twain
> *Pudd'nhead Wilson* [1894]. Pudd'nhead Wilson's Calendar, ch. 5

You have undertaken to cheat me. I won't sue you, for the law is too slow. I'll ruin you.

> Cornelius Vanderbilt
> Letter to former business associates [1853]

I have thought too much to stoop to action!

> Philippe Auguste Villiers de L'Isle-Adam
> *Axel* [1890]

Living? We'll leave that to the servants.

> Villiers de L'Isle-Adam
> Ibid.

The organizer a woman.

> Virgil
> *Aeneid*, bk. I, l. 364

The balance of power.

> Sir Robert Walpole
> Speech in the House of Commons [February 13, 1741]

You can't hold a man down without staying down with him.

Booker T. Washington
Attributed

Inconsistencies of opinion, arising from changes of circumstances, are often justifiable.

Daniel Webster
Speech [July 25 and 27, 1846]

It is a test of true theories not only to account for but to predict phenomena.

William Whewell
Philosophy of the Inductive Sciences
[1840], aphorism 39

Civilization advances by extending the number of important operations which we can perform without thinking about them.

Alfred North Whitehead
An Introduction of Mathematics [1911], ch. 5

O Captain! my Captain! our fearful
   trip is done,
The ship has weather'd every rack,
   the prize we sought is won,
The port is near, the bells I hear, the
   people all exulting.

>Walt Whitman
>"O Captain! My Captain!," st. 1

This book is about the organization
   man. If the term is vague, it is
   because I can think of no other
   way to describe the people I am
   talking about. . . . They are the
   ones of our middle class who
   have left home, spiritually as well
   as physically, to take the vows of
   organization life, and it is they
   who are the mind and soul of our
   great self-perpetuating institu-
   tions.

>William H. Whyte, Jr.
>*The Organization Man* [1956],
>   pt. I, ch. 1

A man cannot be too careful in the
   choice of his enemies.

>Oscar Wilde
>*The Picture of Dorian Gray* [1891],
>   ch. 1

He knew the precise psychological
moment when to say nothing.

> Wilde
> Ibid. ch. 2

There is only one thing in the world
worse than being talked about,
and that is not being talked
about.

> Wilde
> Ibid. ch. 1

We feel that we are greater than we
know.

> William Wordsworth
> *The River Duddon* [1820], sonnet 34,
> Afterthought, l. 14

It takes a wise man to recognize a
wise man.

> Xenophanes
> From Diogenes Laertius, *Lives of Emi-
> nent Philosophers*, Xenophanes, IX

It's certain there is no fine thing
Since Adam's fall but needs much
laboring.

> William Butler Yeats
> *In the Seven Woods* [1904]. Adam's
> Curse, st. 3

Criticism comes easier than crafts-
manship.

Zeuxis
From Pliny the Elder, *Natural History*

Be wise today; 'tis madness to defer.

Edward Young
Night Thoughts [1742–1745].
Night I, l. 390

Money

Draw your salary before spending it.

> George Ade
> *Forty Modern Fables* [1901].
> The People's Choice

Do not count your chickens before they are hatched.

> Aesop
> "The Milkmaid and Her Pail"

It is thrifty to prepare today for the wants of tomorrow.

> Aesop
> "The Ant and the Grasshopper"

Do not set your heart on wealth . . .
Do not strain to seek increases,
What you have, let it suffice you.
If riches come to you by theft,
They will not stay the night with you . . .
They made themselves wings like geese,
And flew away to the sky.

> Amenemope
> *The Instruction of Amenemope*, ch. 7

A fool and his money are soon parted.

> Anonymous English proverb

Keeping up with the Joneses.

> Anonymous popular saying

Paying through the nose.

Anonymous
Popular phrase for excessive payment

Caveat emptor [Let the buyer beware].

Anonymous Latin proverb

I am amazed that anyone who has made a fortune should send for his friends.

Aristophanes
Plutus [c. 388 B.C.],1. 340

When men drink, then they are rich and successful and win lawsuits and are happy and help their friends.
Quickly, bring me a beaker of wine, so that I may wet my mind and say something clever.

Aristophanes
Knights [424 B.C.], 1. 92

Business, you know, may bring money, but friendship hardly ever does.

Jane Austen
Emma [1815], ch. 34

Chiefly the mold of a man's fortune
is in his own hands.

Francis Bacon
Essays [1625]. Of Fortune

Fortune is like the market, where
many times, if you can stay a little, the price will fall.

Bacon
Ibid. Of Delays

If a man look sharply and atten-
tively, he shall see Fortune; for
though she is blind, she is not
invisible.

Bacon
Ibid. Of Fortune

We never understand how little we
need in this world until we know
the loss of it.

Sir James M. Barrie
Margaret Ogilvy [1896], ch. 8

Economic distress will teach men,
if anything can, that realities are
less dangerous than fancies, that
fact-finding is more effective than
fault-finding.

Carl Becker
Progress and Power [1935]

An American credit card . . . is just as good in Europe as American gold used to be.

> Edward Bellamy
> *Looking Backward, 2000–1887* [1888], ch. 13

Equal wealth and equal opportunities of culture . . . have simply made us all members of one class.

> Bellamy
> Ibid. ch. 14

Love of money . . . was the general impulse to effort in your day.

> Bellamy
> Ibid. ch. 9

I'm tired of Love: I'm still more tired of Rhyme.
But Money gives me pleasure all the time.

> Hilaire Belloc
> "Fatigue"

There is no inherent mechanism in our present system which can with certainty prevent competitive sectional bargaining for wages from setting up a vicious spiral of rising prices under full employment.

> Sir William Henry Beveridge
> *Full Employment in a Free Society*
> [1945]

Rich in good works.

> New Testament
> I Timothy 6:18

The love of money is the root of all evil.

> New Testament
> I Timothy 6:10

But if any provide not for his own, and specially for those of his own house, he hath denied the faith, and is worse than an infidel.

> The Bible
> New Testament
> I Timothy 5:8

The Lord reward him according to his works.

> New Testament
> II Timothy 4:14

He that maketh haste to be rich shall not be innocent.

> Old Testament
> Proverbs 28:20

Labor not to be rich: cease from thine own wisdom.

> Old Testament
> Proverbs 23:4

Labor, n. one of the processes by which A acquires property for B.

> Ambrose Bierce
> *The Devil's Dictionary* [1906]

Which of you, intending to build a tower, sitteth not down first, and counteth the cost, whether he have sufficient to finish it?

> New Testament
> Luke 14:28

In the day of prosperity there is a forgetfulness of affliction: and in the day of affliction there is no more remembrance of prosperity.

> Apocrypha
> The Wisdom of Jesus the Son of
>   Sirach, or Ecclesiasticus 11:25

The borrower is servant to the lender.

> Old Testament
> Proverbs 22:7

You never know what is enough
unless you know what is more
than enough.

William Blake
The Marriage of Heaven and Hell
[1790–1793]. Proverbs of Hell, 1. 46

If we had no winter, the spring
would not be so pleasant: if we
did not sometimes taste of adversity, prosperity would not be so
welcome.

Anne Bradstreet
Meditations Divine and Moral [1664],
14

Let us all be happy and live within
our means, even if we have to
borrow the money to do it with.

Charles Farrar Browne [Artemus
Ward]
"Natural History"

Less is more.

Robert Browning
"Andrea del Sarto" [1855],1. 78

In other countries poverty is a mis-
fortune — with us it is a crime.

Edward Bulwer-Lytton
England and the English [1833]

All progress is based upon a universal innate desire on the part of every organism to live beyond its income.

> Samuel Butler
> *Notebooks* [1912]. Life

While the law [of competition] may be sometimes hard for the individual, it is best for the race, because it insures the survival of the fittest in every department. We accept and welcome, therefore, as conditions to which we must accommodate ourselves, great inequality of environment, the concentration of business, industrial and commercial, in the hands of a few, and the law of competition between these, as being not only beneficial, but essential for the future progress of the race.

> Andrew Carnegie
> "Wealth." From the *North American Review* [June 1889]

The surest way to get a thing in this life is to be prepared for doing without it, to the exclusion even of hope,

> Jane Welsh Carlyle

The man who dies . . . rich dies
disgraced.

Carnegie
Ibid.

Even though work stops, expenses
run on.

Cato the Elder
On Agriculture, XXXIX, 2

Surplus wealth is a sacred trust
which its possessor is bound to
administer in his lifetime for the
good of the community.

Carnegie
Ibid.

Upon the sacredness of property
civilization itself depends — the
right of the laborer to his hundred
dollars in the savings bank, and
equally the legal right of the millionaire to his millions.

Carnegie
Ibid.

There are people who have money and people who are rich.

Coco Chanel
Remark

Possession is eleven points in the law.

Colley Cibber
Woman's Wit [1697], act I

Which I have earned with the sweat of my brows.

Miguel de Cervantes
Don Quixote de la Mancha, pt. I
[1605], bk. I, ch. 4

The pulse of modern life is economic and the fundamental principle of economic production is individual independence.

Ch'en Tu-hsiu
The New Youth [December 1916]

A world where nothing is had for
nothing.

> Arthur Hugh Clough
> *The Bothie of Tober-na-Vuolich* [1848],
>   pt. VIII

No graven images may be
Worshipped, except the currency.

> Clough
> "The Latest Decalogue" [1862], l. 3

The savings of many in the hands of
one.

> Eugene V. Debs
> On wealth

Buy an annuity cheap, and make
   your life interesting to yourself
   and everybody else that watches
   the speculation.

> Charles Dickens
> *Martin Chuzzlewit* [1843–1844],
>   ch. 18

I am the only child of parents who
weighed, measured, and priced
everything; for whom what could
not be weighed, measured, and
priced had no existence.

> Dickens
> *Little Dorrit* [1857–1858],
> bk. I, ch. 2

Money and goods are certainly the
best of references.

> Dickens
> *Our Mutual Friend* [1864–1865],
> bk. I, ch. 4

A billion here, a billion there, and
pretty soon you're talking about
real money.

> Everett M. Dirksen
> Attributed

Increased means and increased leisure are the two civilizers of man.

> Benjamin Disraeli
> Speech to the Conservatives of
> Manchester [April 3, 1872]

Business? It's quite simple. It's
other people's money.

> Alexandre Dumas the Younger
> *La Question d'argent* [1857],
> act II, sc. vii

Great men are they who see that spiritual is stronger than any material force, that thoughts rule the world.

> Ralph Waldo Emerson
> *Letters and Social Aims* [1876].
>   Progress and Culture, Phi Beta
>   Kappa Address [July 18, 1876]

I remember riding in a taxi one afternoon between very tall buildings under a mauve and rosy sky; I began to bawl because I had everything I wanted and knew I would never be so happy again.

> F. Scott Fitzgerald
> "My Lost City" [1932]

Money, which represents the prose of life, and which is hardly spoken of in parlors without an apology, is, in its effects and laws, as beautiful as roses.

> Emerson
> *Essays: Second Series* [1844]. Nominalist and Realist.

Let me tell you about the very rich.
They are different from you and
me. They possess and enjoy early,
and it does something to them,
makes them soft where we are
hard, and cynical where we are
trustful.

>   Fitzgerald
>   *The Rich Boy* [1926]

The victor belongs to the spoils.

>   Fitzgerald
>   *The Beautiful and Damned* [1922]

Human felicity is produced not so
much by great pieces of good fortune that seldom happen, as by
little advantages that occur every
day.

>   Benjamin Franklin
>   *Autobiography* [1731–1759], ch. 9

Remember that time is money.

>   Franklin
>   "Advice to a Young Tradesman" [1748]

When the well's dry, we know the
worth of water.

>   Franklin
>   *Poor Richard's Almanac* [1746]. January

Freedom in economic arrangements is itself a component of freedom broadly understood, so economic freedom is an end in itself. . . . Economic freedom is also an indispensable means toward the achievement of political freedom.

Milton Friedman
Capitalism and Freedom [1962], ch. 1

Positive economics is in principle independent of any particular ethical position or normative judgments. . . . In short, positive economics is or can be an "objective" science.

Friedman
Essays in Positive Economics [1953],
pt. I, 1

There's no such thing as a free lunch.

Friedman
Attributed

One can relish the varied idiocy of human action during a panic to the full, for, while it is a time of great tragedy, nothing is being lost but money.

John Kenneth Galbraith
The Great Crash, 1929 [1955], ch. 1

The individual serves the industrial system not by supplying it with savings and the resulting capital; he serves it by consuming its products.

>   Galbraith
>   *The New Industrial State* [1967], ch. 4

Wealth is not without its advantages and the case to the contrary, although it has often been made, has never proved widely persuasive.

>   Galbraith
>   *The Affluent Society* [1958], ch 1

So long as all the increased wealth which modern progress brings goes but to build up great fortunes, to increase luxury and make sharper the contrast between the House of Have and the House of Want, progress is not real and cannot be permanent.

>   Henry George
>   *Progress and Poverty* [1879]. Introductory: The Problem

The labor of women in the house, certainly, enables men to produce more wealth than they otherwise could; and in this way women are economic factors in society. But so are horses.

Charlotte Perkins Gilman
Women and Economics [1898], ch. 1

America, the land of unlimited possibilities.

Ludwig Max Goldberger
Land of Unlimited Possibilities: Observations on Economic Life in the United States of America [1903]

The illusion that times that were are better than those that are, has probably pervaded all ages.

Horace Greeley
The American Conflict [1864–1866]

This is the unspoken contract of a wife and her works. In the long run wives are to be paid in a peculiar coin — consideration for their feelings. And it usually turns out this is an enormous, unthinkable inflation few men will remit, or if they will, only with a sense of being overcharged.

> Elizabeth Hardwick
> *Seduction and Betrayal: Women in*
>   *Literature* [1974]. Amateurs

[The great economists] can be called the worldly philosophers, for they sought to embrace in a scheme of philosophy the most worldly of all of man's activities — his drive for wealth.

> Robert L. Heilbroner
> *The Worldly Philosophers* [1953].
>   Introduction

Boredom is the keynote of poverty . . . for where there is no money there is no change of any kind, not of scene or of routine.

> Moss Hart
> *Act One* [1959], pt. I

I know on which side my bread is buttered.

> John Heywood
> *Proverbs* [1546], pt. II, ch. 7

Put not your trust in money, but put your money in trust.

> Oliver Wendell Holmes
> *The Autocrat of the Breakfast-Table*
> [1858], ch. 2

He wins every hand who mingles profit with pleasure, by delighting and instructing the reader at the same time.

> Horace
> Ibid. bk. III, l. 343

There is nothing so well known as that we should not expect something for nothing — but we all do and call it Hope.

> Edgar Watson Howe
> *Country Town Sayings* [1911]

For joys fall not to the rich alone, nor has he lived ill, who from birth to death has passed unknown.

> Horace
> *Epistles,* bk. I, epistle xvii, 1. 9

Make money, money by fair means if you can, if not, by any means money.

> Horace
> Ibid. bk. I, epistle i, 1. 66

When a fellow says it hain't the money but the principle o' the thing, it's th' money.

> Frank Hubbard [Abe Martin]
> *Hoss Sense and Nonsense* [1926]

The almighty dollar, that great object of universal devotion throughout our land.

> Washington Irving
> *Wolfert's Roost* [1855]. The Creole Village

The moral flabbiness born of the exclusive worship of the bitch-goddess SUCCESS. That — with the squalid cash interpretation put on the word success — is our national disease.

> James
> *The Letters of William James* [1920]. To H. G. Wells, September 11, 1906

In its widest possible sense, however, a man's Self is the sum total of all that he *can* call his, not only his body and his psychic powers, but his clothes and his house, his wife and children, his ancestors and friends, his reputation and works, his lands and horses, and yacht and bank account. All these things give him the same emotions. If they wax and prosper, he feels triumphant; if they dwindle and die away, he feels cast down.

> William James
> *The Principles of Psychology* [1890], ch. 10

We all live in a state of ambitious
poverty.

> Juvenal
> Ibid. III, l. 182

You Can't Take It with You.

> George S. Kaufman and Moss Hart
> Title of play [1936]

The engine which drives Enterprise
is not Thrift, but Profit.

> Keynes
> *A Treatise on Money* [1930]

It is not easy for men to rise whose
qualities are thwarted by poverty.

> Juvenal
> *Satires*, III, l. 164

There's nothing surer,
The rich get rich and the poor get
poorer,
In the meantime, in between time,
Ain't we got fun.

> Gus Kahn and Raymond B. Egan
> "Ain't We Got Fun" [1920]

Of the maxims of orthodox finance,
none, surely, is more antisocial
than the fetish of liquidity. . . . It
forgets that there is no such thing
as liquidity of investment for the
community as a whole.

> John Maynard Keynes
> *The General Theory of Employment,
> Interest and Money* [1936], ch. 12

The love of money as a possession — as distinguished from the
love of money as a means to the
enjoyments and realities of life —
will be recognized for what it is, a
somewhat disgusting morbidity,
one of those semi-criminal, semi-
pathological propensities which
one hands over with a shudder to
the specialists in mental disease.

Keynes
Essay in Persuasion [1931], pt. V

There are no intrinsic reasons for
the scarcity of capital.

Keynes
*The General Theory of Employment,
Interest and Money* [1936], ch. 24

Wealth and children are the adorn-
ment of this present life: but good
works, which are lasting, are better in the sight of thy Lord as to
recompense, and better as to
hope.

The Koran
Chapter 18:46

The human species, according to
the best theory I can form of it, is
composed of two distinct races,
the men who borrow, and the
men who lend.

Charles Lamb
Essays of Elia [1823]. The Two Races
of Men

The gratitude of most men is merely a secret desire to receive greater benefits.

> François, Duc de La Rochefoucauld
> *Reflections; or, Sentences and Moral Maxims* [1678], maxim 298

We need greater virtues to sustain good fortune than bad.

> La Rochefoucauld
> Ibid. maxim 25

I cried all the way to the bank.

> Liberace
> *Liberace: An Autobiography* [1973], ch. 2

Labor is prior to, and independent of, capital. Capital is only the fruit of labor, and could never have existed if labor had not first existed. Labor is the superior of capital, and deserves much the higher consideration. Capital has its rights, which are as worthy of protection as any other rights.

> Abraham Lincoln
> First Annual Message to Congress [December 3, 1861]

Anticipate charity by preventing poverty; assist the reduced fellow-man, either by a considerable gift, or a sum of money, or by teaching him a trade, or by putting him in the way of business, so that he may earn an honest livelihood, and not be forced to the dreadful alternative of holding out his hand for charity. This is the highest step and the summit of charity's golden ladder.

Maimonides
Charity's Eight Degrees

When commercial capital occupies a position of unquestioned ascendancy, it everywhere constitutes a system of plunder.

Karl Marx
Capital [1867–1883], pt. II, ch. 21

Of all the classes that stand face to face with the bourgeoisie today, the proletariat alone is a really revolutionary class. The other classes decay and finally disappear in the race of modern industry; the proletariat is its special and essential product.

Karl Marx and Friedrich Engels
The Communist Manifesto, sec. 1

The bourgeoisie, by the rapid improvement of all instruments of production, by the immensely facilitated means of communication, draws all, even the most barbarian, nations into civilization.

> Marx and Engels
> Ibid.

Riches cover a multitude of woes.

> Menander
> *The Boeotian Girl*, fragment 90

Everybody thinks of economics whether he is aware of it or not. In joining a political party and in casting his ballot, the citizen implicitly takes a stand upon essential economic theories.

> Ludwig Edler von Mises
> *Human Action* [1949]

There is nothing so degrading as the constant anxiety about one's means of livelihood. . . . Money is like a sixth sense without which you cannot make a complete use of the other five.

> W. Somerset Maugham
> *Of Human Bondage* [1915], ch. 51

No one in this world, so far as I know . . . has ever lost money by underestimating the intelligence of the great masses of the plain people.

> H. L. Mencken
> Notes on journalism, *Chicago Tribune*
> [September 19, 1926]

The market economy as such does not respect political frontiers. Its field is the world.

> Mises
> Ibid.

Give us the luxuries of life, and we will dispense with its necessaries.

> John Lothrop Motley
> Quoted in Oliver Wendell Holmes,
> *The Autocrat of the Breakfast-Table*
> [1858], ch. 6

Statistical figures referring to economic events are historical data. They tell us what happened in a nonrepeatable historical case.

> Mises
> Ibid.

What I mean by Socialism is a condition of society in which there should be neither rich nor poor, neither master nor master's man, neither idle nor overworked, neither brain-sick brain workers nor heart-sick hand workers, in a word, in which all men would be living in equality of condition, and would manage their affairs unwastefully, and with the full consciousness that harm to one would mean harm to all — the realization at last of the meaning of the word *commonwealth*.

> William Morris
> Written for *Justice* [1884]

A business with an income at its
   heels
Furnishes always oil for its own
   wheels.

> Motoori Norinaga
> "Retirement" [1782], l. 615

Money does not pay for anything,
   never has, never will. It is an economic axiom as old as the hills
   that goods and services can be
   paid for only with goods and services.

> Albert Jay Nock
> *Memoirs of a Superfluous Man* [1943],
>   ch. 13, 3

Private property is a natural fruit of
   labor, a product of intense activity of man, acquired through his
   energetic determination to ensure
   and develop with his own
   strength his own existence and
   that of his family, and to create
   for himself and his own an existence of just freedom, not only
   economic, but also political, cul-
   tural and religious.

> Pope Pius XII
> Radio broadcast [September 1, 1944]

When there is an income tax, the
   just man will pay more and the
   unjust less on the same amount
   of income.

> Plato
> *The Republic*, bk. I, 343–D

Get place and wealth, if possible
    with grace;
If not, by any means get wealth and
    place.

> Alexander Pope
> *Imitations of Horace* [1733–1738],
>   epistle I, bk. I, l. 103

Everything is worth what its pur-
    chaser will pay for it.

> Publilius Syrus
> Maxim 847

Labor, like all other things which
    are purchased and sold, and
    which may be increased or dimin-
    ished in quantity, has its natural
    and its market price. The natural
    price of labor is that price which
    is necessary to enable the labor-
    ers, one with another, to subsist
    and perpetuate their race, with-
    out either increase or diminution.

> David Ricardo
> *On the Principles of Political Economy
>   and Taxation* [1817], ch. 5

There are occasions when it is un-
    doubtedly better to incur loss
    than to make gain.

> Plautus
> *Captivi,* act II, sc. ii, l. 77

A good reputation is more valuable
    than money.

> Publilius Syrus
> Maxim 108

Money begets money.

> John Ray
> *English Proverbs* [1670]

The ripest peach is highest on the tree.

> James Whitcomb Riley
> "The Ripest Peach," st. 1

Out of this modern civilization economic royalists carved new dynasties. . . . The royalists of the economic order have conceded that political freedom was the business of the Government, but they have maintained that economic slavery was nobody's business.

> Franklin D. Roosevelt
> Speech accepting renomination
> [June 27, 1936]

There is no way of keeping profits up but by keeping wages down.

> Ricardo
> *On Protection to Agriculture* [1820],
> sec. 6

God gave me my money. I believe the power to make money is a gift from God. . . . I believe it is my duty to make money and still more money and to use the money I make for the good of my fellow man according to the dictates of my conscience.

> John D. Rockefeller
> In an interview [1905]

These unhappy times call for the building of plans . . . that build from the bottom up and not from the top down, that put their faith once more in the forgotten man at the bottom of the economic pyramid.

> Roosevelt
> Radio address [April 7, 1932]

Always try to rub up against money, for if you rub up against money long enough, some of it may rub off on you.

> Damon Runyon
> *Guys and Dolls* [1931]. A Very Honorable Guy

The test of our progress is not whether we add more to the abundance of those who have much; it is whether we provide enough for those who have too little.

> Roosevelt
> Second Inaugural Address
> [January 20, 1937]

Money is the seed of money, and the first guinea is sometimes more difficult to acquire than the second million.

> Jean Jacques Rousseau
> *Discourse upon the Origin and Foundation of the Inequality Among Mankind* [1754]

Every increased possession loads us
with a new weariness.

> Ruskin
> *The Eagle's Nest* [1872], ch. 5

In truth, prosperity tries the souls
even of the wise.

> Sallust
> *The War with Catiline*, sec. 11

I like to walk about amidst the
beautiful things that adorn the
world; but private wealth I should
decline, or any sort of personal
possessions, because they would
take away my liberty.

> George Santayana
> *Soliloquies in England and Later Solilo-
> quies* [1922]. The Irony of Liberalism

Borrowers are nearly always ill-
spenders, and it is with lent
money that all evil is mainly done
and all unjust war protracted.

> John Ruskin
> *The Crown of Wild Olive* [1866],
> lecture 1

Value is the life-giving power of
anything; cost, the quantity of
labor required to produce it;
price, the quantity of labor which
its possessor will take in exchange
for it.

> Ruskin
> *Munera Pulveris* [1862], ch. 1

Charity degrades those who receive
it and hardens those who dispense it.

> George Sand
> *Consuelo* [1842]

Man is not the sum of what he has
but the totality of what he does
not yet have, of what he might
have.

Jean Paul Sartre
Situations [1939], I

Capitalism inevitably and by virtue
of the very logic of its civilization
creates, educates and subsidizes a
vested interest in social unrest.

Joseph Alois Schumpeter
Capitalism, Socialism and Democracy
[1942], ch. 13

It is not the man who has too little,
but the man who craves more,
that is poor.

Seneca
Epistles 2, 2

He is well paid that is well satisfied.

William Shakespeare
The Merchant of Venice, act IV, sc. i,
l. 416

No profit grows where is no pleasure ta'en;
In brief, sir, study what you most affect.

Shakespeare
The Taming of the Shrew, act I, sc. i,
l. 39

Thou art not for the fashion of
these times,
Where none will sweat but for promotion.

Shakespeare
As You Like It, act II, sc. iii, l. 59

To seek their fortunes further than
at home,
Where small experience grows.

Shakespeare
The Taming of the Shrew, act I, sc. ii,
l. 51

Put money in thy purse.

Shakespeare
Othello, act I, sc. iii, l. 345

Mend your speech a little,
Lest you may mar your fortunes.

Shakespeare
King Lear, act I, sc. i, l. 96

No man's pie is freed
From his ambitious finger.

> Shakespeare
> *King Henry the Eighth*, act I, sc. i, 1. 52

I am a Millionaire. That is my religion.

> George Bernard Shaw
> *Major Barbara* [1905], act II

Consumption is the sole end and
purpose of all production; and the
interest of the producer ought to
be attended to only so far as it
may be necessary for promoting
that of the consumer.

> Adam Smith
> *An Inquiry into the Nature and Causes
> of the Wealth of Nations* [1776], vol.
> II, bk. IV, ch. 8

Solvency is entirely a matter of temperament and not of income .

> Logan Pearsall Smith
> *Afterthoughts* [1931]

There are few sorrows, however
poignant, in which a good income
is of no avail.

> Smith
> Ibid.

Money: There's nothing in the world so demoralizing as money.

> Sophocles
> *Antigone* [c. 442 B.C.], l. 295

Greed is good! Greed is right! Greed works! Greed will save the U.S.A.!

> Oliver Stone
> *Wall Street* (screenplay) [1987]

I won't quarrel with my bread and butter.

> Jonathan Swift
> *Polite Conversation* [1738], dialogue 1

Let all the learned say what they can,
'Tis ready money makes the man.

> William Somerville
> "Ready Money" [1727]

None of us really understands what's going on with all these numbers.

> David Stockman
> On the U.S. budget [1981]

The elegant simplicity of the three per cents.

> William Scott, Lord Stowell
> From Campbell, *Lives of the Lord Chancellors* [1857], vol. X, ch. 212

Moderation in all things.

Terence
Andria (*The Lady of Andros*), l. 61

I know of no country, indeed, where the love of money has taken stronger hold on the affections of men and where a profounder contempt is expressed for the theory of the permanent equality of property.

Alexis de Tocqueville
Democracy in America, pt. I [1835], ch. 3

Industrialized communities neglect the very objects for which it is worth while to acquire riches in their feverish preoccupation with the means by which riches can be acquired.

Richard Tawney
The Acquisitive Society [1920]

That man is the richest whose pleasures are the cheapest.

Henry David Thoreau
Journal [1906], March 11,1856

The more is given the less the people will work for themselves, and the less they work the more their poverty will increase.

Leo Tolstoi
Help for the Starving, pt. III [January 1892]

Always remember . . . that when you go into an attorney's office door, you will have to pay for it, first or last.

> Anthony Trollope
> *The Last Chronicle of Barset* [1867],
> vol. I, ch. 20

I have been poor and I have been rich. Rich is better.

> Sophie Tucker
> Attributed

This is the happiest of all men, for he is superior to everything he possesses.

> Voltaire
> *Candide* [1759], ch. 25

The rich rob the poor and the poor rob one another.

> Sojourner Truth
> Saying

Conspicuous consumption of valuable goods is a means of reputability to the gentleman of leisure.

> Thorstein Veblen
> *The Theory of the Leisure Class* [1899],
> ch. 4

A man is never so on trial as in the moment of excessive good fortune.

> Lew Wallace
> *Ben Hur: A Tale of the Christ* [1880],
> bk. V, ch. 7

All those men have their price.

> Sir Robert Walpole
> From William Coxe, *Memoirs of Walpole* [1798], vol. IV, p. 369

Labor in this country is independent and proud. It has not to ask the patronage of capital, but capital solicits the aid of labor.

> Daniel Webster
> Speech [April 2, 1824]

Nowadays we are all of us so hard up that the only pleasant things to pay are compliments. They're the only things we can pay.

> Oscar Wilde
> *Lady Windermere's Fan* [1892], act I

No man can lose what he never had.

> Izaak Walton
> *The Compleat Angler* [1653–1655], pt. I, ch. 5

Attorney-General Sir John Holker: The labor of two days, then, is that for which you ask two hundred guineas?
Whistler: No — I ask it for the knowledge of a lifetime.

> James McNeill Whistler
> *The Gentle Art of Making Enemies* [1890]. Messieurs Les Enemis

Motivation

The best you get is an even break.

Franklin Pierce Adams
"Ballade of Schopenhauer's Philosophy"

No one means all he says, and yet
very few say all they mean, for
words are slippery and thought is
viscous.

Adams
Ibid. ch. 31

To be ignorant of one's ignorance is
the malady of the ignorant.

Bronson Alcott
Table Talk [1877]. Discourse

All experience is an arch, to build
upon.

Henry Adams
The Education of Henry Adams [1907],
ch. 6

Slow and steady wins the race.

Aesop
"The Hare and the Tortoise"

Eighty percent of success is show-
ing up.

Woody Allen
Interview

Climb high
Climb far
Your goal the sky
Your aim the star.

> Anonymous
> Inscription on Hopkins Memorial
>   Steps, Williams College, Williams-
>   town, Massachusetts

Count that day lost whose low
   descending sun
Views from thy hand no worthy
   action done.

> Anonymous saying

I've been working on the railroad
All the livelong day,
I've been working on the railroad
To pass the time away.
Don't you hear the whistle blowing?
Rise up so early in the morn.
Don't you hear the captain shouting,
"Dinah blow your horn."

> Anonymous
> "I've Been Working on the Railroad"

Man may work from sun to sun,
But woman's work is never done.

> Anonymous saying

Oh, why don't you work
Like other men do?
How the hell can I work
When there's no work to do?

> Anonymous
> "Hallelujah, I'm a Bum" [c. 1907]

Though little, I'll work as hard as a
    Turk,
If you'll give me employ,
To plow and sow, and reap and mow,
And be a farmer's boy.

> Anonymous
> "The Farmer's Boy" [before 1689], st. 2

"Murphy's Law": If anything can go
    wrong, it will.

> Anonymous saying [1950s]

Dirty work at the crossroads.

> Anonymous
> Attributed to Walter Melville's melo-
> drama *The Girl Who Took the Wrong
> Turning; or, No Wedding Bells for
> Him*

Don't cross the bridge until you
    come to it.

> Anonymous proverb

I seen my duty and I done it.

> Anonymous saying [current since the
> 19th century]

It's all in the day's work.

> Anonymous saying [current since the 18th century]

The difficult we do immediately. The impossible takes a little longer.

> Anonymous
> Slogan of United States Army Service Forces

Time is of the essence.

> Anonymous saying

Haste, haste, has no blessing.

> Anonymous African proverb (Swahili)

Parvis e glandibus quercus [Tall oaks from little acorns grow].

> Anonymous Latin saying

Let each man exercise the art he knows.

> Aristophanes
> *Wasps* [422 B.C.], 1.1431

For the things we have to learn before we can do them, we learn by doing them.

> Aristotle
> *Nicomachean Ethics,* bk. II, ch. 1

It is possible to fail in many ways
   . . . while to succeed is possible
   only in one way (for which reason
   also one is easy and the other
   difficult — to miss the mark easy,
   to hit it difficult).

> Aristotle
> Ibid. ch. 6

Well begun is half done.

> Aristotle
> *Politics,* bk. V, ch. 4

We do not what we ought;
What we ought not, we do;
And lean upon the thought
That chance will bring us through.

> Matthew Arnold
> *Empedocles on Etna* [1852], act I, sc. ii,
> 1. 237

Conduct is three-fourths of our life
   and its largest concern.

> Arnold
> *Literature and Dogma* [1873], ch. 1

Greatness is a spiritual condition
   worthy to excite love, interest,
   and admiration.

> Arnold
> *Culture and Anarchy* [1869]. Sweet-
> ness and Light.

He who works for sweetness and
   light united, works to make reason and the will of God prevail.

> Arnold
> Ibid.

What actions are the most excellent? Those, certainly, which
   most powerfully appeal to the
   great primary human affections:
   to those elementary feelings
   which subsist permanently in the
   race, and which are independent
   of time. These feelings are permanent and the same; that which
   interests them is permanent and
   the same also.

> Arnold
> Preface to *Poems* [1853]

Well done is quickly done.

> Augustus Caesar
> From Suetonius, *Augustus*, sec. 25

Knowledge is power [Nam et ipsa
   scientia potestas est].

> Francis Bacon
> *Meditationes Sacrae* [1597].
>   De Haeresibus

Revenge is a kind of wild justice,
    which the more man's nature
    runs to, the more ought law to
    weed it out.

>   Bacon
>   *Essays* [1625]. Of Revenge

There can be no progress (real, that
    is, moral) except in the individual
    and by the individual himself.

>   Charles Baudelaire
>   *Mon Coeur mis à nu* [1887], XV

A great many people have come up
    to me and asked me how I man-
    age to get so much work done and
    still keep looking so dissipated.
    My answer is "Don't you wish you
    knew?"

>   Robert Benchley
>   *How to Get Things Done*

The monuments of wit survive the
    monuments of power.

>   Bacon
>   *Essex's Device* [1595]

If you are mediocre and you grovel,
    you shall succeed.

>   Pierre de Beaumarchais
>   *Le Mariage de Figaro* [1784],
>   act III, sc. iii

You've got to get up, you've got to
   get up,
You've got to get up this morning!

>   Irving Berlin
>   "Oh! How I Hate to Get Up in the
>   Morning" [1918]

Anything You Can Do, I Can Do
   Better.

>   Berlin
>   *Annie Get Your Gun* [1946],
>   title of song

Observation is a passive science,
   experimentation an active science.

>   Claude Bernard
>   *Introduction à l'étude de la médecine
>   expérimentale* [1865]

Better one's own duty, [though]
   imperfect,
Than another's duty well performed.

>   Bhagavad Gita
>   Chapter 3, verse 35, and ch. 18, v. 47

A workman that needeth not to be
   ashamed.

>   The Bible
>   New Testament
>   II Timothy 2:15

Be sober, be vigilant; because your adversary the devil, as a roaring lion, walketh about, seeking whom he may devour.

New Testament
Peter 5:8

God hath chosen the foolish things of the world to confound the wise; and God hath chosen the weak things of the world to confound the things which are mighty.

New Testament
I Corinthians 1:27

Every man's work shall be made manifest: for the day shall declare it, because it shall be revealed by fire; and the fire shall try every man's work of what sort it is.

New Testament
I Corinthians 3:13

I have fought a good fight, I have finished my course, I have kept the faith.

New Testament
II Timothy 4:7

Labor of love.

> New Testament
> I Thessalonians 1:3

Let all things be done decently and in order.

> New Testament
> II Corinthians 14:40

No man can serve two masters: for either he will hate the one, and love the other; or else he will hold to the one, and despise the other. Ye cannot serve God and mammon.

> New Testament
> Matthew 6:24

Study to be quiet, and to do your own business.

> New Testament
> I Thessalonians 4:11

That thou doest, do quickly.

> New Testament
> John 13:27

The Father, who without respect of persons judgeth according to every man's work.

> New Testament
> I Peter 1:17

The disciple is not above his master, nor the servant above his lord.

> New Testament
> Matthew 10:24

This one thing I do, forgetting those things which are behind, and reaching forth unto those things which are before,
I press toward the mark.

> New Testament
> Philippians 3:13–14

Consider that I labored not for myself only, but for all them that seek learning.

> Apocrypha
> The Wisdom of Jesus the Son of
> Sirach, or Ecclesiasticus 33:17

The laborer is worthy of his hire.

> New Testament
> Luke 10:7

Whosoever will save his life shall lose it: and whosoever will lose his life for my sake shall find it.
For what is a man profited, if he shall gain the whole world, and lose his own soul?

> New Testament
> Matthew 16:25–26

Go to the ant, thou sluggard; consider her ways, and be wise:
Which having no guide, overseer, or
ruler,
Provideth her meat in the summer,
and gathereth her food in the har-
vest.

> Old Testament
> Proverbs 6:6–8

In all labor there is profit: but the
talk of the lips tendeth only to
penury.

> Old Testament
> Proverbs 14:23

Many shall run to and fro, and
knowledge shall be increased.

> Old Testament
> Daniel 12:4

Seek not out the things that are too
hard for thee, neither search the
things that are above thy strength.

> Apocrypha
> The Wisdom of Jesus the Son of
> Sirach, or Ecclesiasticus 3:21

Seest thou a man diligent in his
business? He shall stand before
kings.

> Old Testament
> Proverbs 22:29

The desire accomplished is sweet to the soul.

Old Testament
Proverbs 13:19

To every thing there is a season, and a time to every purpose under the heaven.
A time to be born, and a time to die; a time to plant, and a time to pluck up that which is planted;
A time to kill, and a time to heal; a time to break down, and a time to build up;
A time to weep, and a time to laugh; a time to mourn, and a time to dance;
A time to cast away stones, and a time to gather stones together; a time to embrace, and a time to refrain from embracing;
A time to get, and a time to lose; a time to keep, and a time to cast away;
A time to rend, and a time to sew; a time to keep silence, and a time to speak;
A time to love, and a time to hate; a time of war, and a time of peace.

Old Testament
Ecclesiastes 3:1–8

Whatsoever thy hand findeth to do,
do it with thy might; for there is
no work, nor device, nor knowledge, nor wisdom, in the grave,
whither thou goest.

> Old Testament
> Ecclesiastes 9:10

Achievement, n. the death of endeavor and the birth of disgust.

> Ambrose Bierce
> *The Devil's Dictionary* [1906]

Your old men shall dream dreams,
your young men shall see visions.

> Old Testament
> Joel 2:28

Great things are done when men
and mountains meet;
This is not done by jostling in the
street.

> William Blake
> Poems [written c. 1807–1809] from
> Blake's Notebook. Great Things Are
> Done

Improvement makes straight roads;
but the crooked roads without
improvement are roads of genius.

Blake
The Marriage of Heaven and Hell
[1790–1793]. Proverbs of Hell, l. 66

The terrible burden of having nothing to do.

Nicolas Boileau-Despréaux
Epistle 11

No bird soars too high, if he soars
with his own wings.

Blake
Ibid. l. 15

Sore laborers have hard hands and
old sinners have brawny con-
sciences.

Anne Bradstreet
Meditations Divine and Moral [1664],
36

There is in most Americans some spark of idealism, which can be fanned into a flame. It takes sometimes a divining rod to find what it is; but when found, and that means often, when disclosed to the owners, the results are often most extraordinary.

Louis D. Brandeis
The Words of Justice Brandeis [1953]

A minute's success pays the failure of years.

Browning
"Apollo and the Fates" [1886], st. 42

'Tis not what man does which exalts him, but what man would do!

Robert Browning
Saul [1855], st. 18

No work begun shall ever pause for death!

Browning
The Ring and the Book [1868–1869],
bk. VII, Pompilia, l. 1787

We find great things are made of
    little things,
And little things go lessening till at
    last
Comes God behind them.

> Browning
> "Mr. Sludge, 'The Medium' " [1864],
>   l. 1112

What I aspired to be,
And was not, comforts me.

> Browning
> *Rabbi Ben Ezra* [1864], st. 7

To most people nothing is more
    troublesome than the effort of
    thinking.

> James Bryce
> *Studies in History and Jurisprudence*
> [1901]. Obedience

There are two days in the week
    about which and upon which I
    never worry. Two carefree days,
    kept sacredly free from fear and
    apprehension. One of these days
    is Yesterday. . . . And the other
    day I do not worry about is To-
    morrow.

> Robert Jones Burdette
> *The Golden Day*

Do what thy manhood bids thee do,
    from none but self expect ap-
    plause;
He noblest lives and noblest dies
    who makes and keeps his self-
    made laws.

> Sir Richard Burton
> *The Kasîdah of Haji Abdû El-Yazdi,*
>   pt. VIII, st. 37

Be not solitary, be not idle.

> Robert Burton
> *The Anatomy of Melancholy* [1621–
>   1651], pt. III, sec. 4, member 2,
>   subsec. 6

Birds of a feather will gather to-
    gether.

> Burton
> Ibid. sec. 1, member 1, subsec. 2

No rule is so general, which admits
    not some exception.

> Burton
> Ibid. pt. I, sec. 2, member 2, subsec. 3

Seneca thinks the gods are well pleased when they see great men contending with adversity.

> Burton
> Ibid. pt. II, sec. 2, member 1, subsec. 1

It is far safer to know too little than too much. People will condemn the one, though they will resent being called upon to exert themselves to follow the other.

> Samuel Butler
> *The Way of All Flesh* [1903], ch. 5

Every man's work, whether it be literature or music or pictures or architecture or anything else, is always a portrait of himself.

> Butler
> Ibid. ch. 14

The man who lets himself be bored is even more contemptible than the bore.

> Butler
> *The Fair Haven* [1873]. Memoir, ch. 3

A man must serve his time to every
   trade
Save censure — critics all are ready-
   made.

> Lord Byron
> *English Bards and Scotch Reviewers*
>   [1809], l. 63

Even good men like to make the
   public stare.

> Lord Byron
> *Don Juan* [1821], canto III, st. 81

Fame is the thirst of youth.

> Lord Byron
> *Childe Harold's Pilgrimage*, canto III
>   [1816], st. 112

Such hath it been — shall be —
   beneath the sun
The many still must labor for the one.

> Lord Byron
> *The Corsair* [1814], canto I, st. 8

The world is a bundle of hay,
Mankind are the asses that pull,
Each tugs in a different way —
And the greatest of all is John Bull!

> Lord Byron
> Letter to Thomas Moore [June 22,
>   1821]

But whether it be dream or truth, to do well is what matters. If it be truth, for truth's sake. If not, then to gain friends for the time when we awaken.

Pedro Calderón de la Barca
Life Is a Dream, act III, 236

The struggle to reach the top is itself enough to fulfill the heart of man. One must believe that Sisyphus is happy.

Albert Camus
The Myth of Sisyphus (*Le Mythe de Sisyphe*) [1942]

So here hath been dawning
Another blue day:
Think, wilt thou let it
Slip useless away?

Thomas Carlyle
"Today"

All work is as seed sown; it grows and spreads, and sows itself anew.

Carlyle
On Boswell's *Life of Johnson* [1832]

Man is a tool-using animal. . . .
   Without tools he is nothing, with
   tools he is all.

> Carlyle
> *Sartor Resartus* [1833–1834],
>   bk. I, ch. 5

No man lives without jostling and
   being jostled; in all ways he has to
   elbow himself through the world,
   giving and receiving offense.

> Carlyle
> *Critical and Miscellaneous Essays*
>   [1839–1857]. Sir Walter Scott

The great law of culture is: Let each
   become all that he was created
   capable of being.

> Carlyle
> Ibid. Richter

There is endless merit in a man's
   knowing when to have done.

> Carlyle
> *Francia* [1845]

Begin at the beginning . . . and go
   on till you come to the end: then
   stop.

> Lewis Carroll
> *Alice's Adventures in Wonderland*
>   [1865], ch. 12

And though hard be the task,
"Keep a stiff upper lip."

> Phoebe Cary
> "Keep a Stiff Upper Lip"

That is happiness; to be dissolved
into something complete and
great.

> Willa Cather
> *My Ántonia* [1918], bk. I, ch. 2

An honest man's word is as good as
his bond.

> Miguel de Cervantes
> *Don Quixote de la Mancha,* pt. II
> [1615], bk. IV, ch. 34

Diligence is the mother of good
fortune.

> Cervantes
> Ibid. 38

Honesty's the best policy.

> Cervantes
> Ibid. bk. III, ch. 33

Let every man mind his own business.

> Cervantes
> Ibid. pt. I [1605], bk. III, ch. 8

The ass will carry his load, but not a
   double load; ride not a free horse
   to death.

> Cervantes
> Ibid. pt. II, bk. IV, ch. 71

The proof of the pudding is in the
   eating.

> Cervantes
> Ibid. pt. I, bk. IV, ch. 10

How many cares one loses when
   one decides not to be something
   but to be someone.

> Coco Chanel
> Remark

You get the satisfaction of being
   heard, and that is the whole possible scope of human ambition.

> John Jay Chapman
> *Learning and Other Essays* [1910]. The
>   Unity of Human Nature

Viva la huelga [Long live the strike]!

> Cesar Chavez
> Slogan of the United Farm Workers
>   [the 1960s]

Man's happiness in life is the result of man's own effort and is neither the gift of God nor a spontaneous natural product.

> Ch'en Tu-hsiu
> *The New Youth* [February 1918]

Dispatch is the soul of business.

> Philip Dormer Stanhope, Earl of Chesterfield
> *Letters to His Son* [1774]. February 5, 1750

Idleness is only the refuge of weak minds.

> Lord Chesterfield
> Ibid. July 20, 1749

Whatever is worth doing at all, is worth doing well.

> Lord Chesterfield
> Ibid. March 10, 1746

Everyone has his day and some days last longer than others.

> Winston Churchill
> Speech in the House of Commons [January 1952]

I have nothing to offer but blood, toil, tears and sweat.

> Churchill
> First Statement as Prime Minister, House of Commons [May 13, 1940]

You're either part of the solution or
part of the problem.

> Eldridge Cleaver
> Speech, San Francisco [1968]

Learning without thought is labor
lost; thought without learning is
perilous.

> Confucius
> *The Confucian Analects* 2:15

Never give in, never give in, never,
never, never, never — in nothing,
great or small, large or petty —
never give in except to convictions of honor and good sense.

> Churchill
> Address at Harrow School
> [October 29, 1941]

Work without Hope draws nectar in
a sieve,
And Hope without an object cannot
live.

> Samuel Taylor Coleridge
> "Work Without Hope" [February 21,
> 1825], l. 13

The superior man . . . does not set his mind either for anything, or against anything; what is right he will follow.

> Confucius
> Ibid. 4:10

Do your duty, and leave the rest to heaven.

> Pierre Corneille
> *Horace* [1639], act II, sc. viii

The man of virtue makes the difficulty to be overcome his first business, and success only a subsequent consideration.

> Confucius
> Ibid. 6:20

I don't like work — no man does — but I like what is in work — the chance to find yourself. Your own reality — for yourself, not for others — what no other man can ever know.

> Joseph Conrad
> *Heart of Darkness* [1902], I

Every day, in every way, I'm getting better and better.

> Emile Coué
> Formula of his faith cures, inscribed in his sanitarium, Nancy, France

Absence of occupation is not rest,
A mind quite vacant is a mind distress'd.

> William Cowper
> *Retirement,* l. 623

Six days shalt thou labor and do all
thou art able,
And on the seventh — holystone the
decks and scrape the cable.

> Richard Henry Dana
> *Two Years Before the Mast* [1840], ch. 3

He listens well who takes notes.

> Dante
> Ibid. Inferno, canto XV, l. 99

Those who aim at great deeds must
also suffer greatly.

> Crassus
> From Plutarch, *Lives,* Crassus, ch. 26

Go right on and listen as thou goest.

> Dante
> *The Divine Comedy* [c. 1310–1321].
> Purgatorio, canto V, I. 45

If thou follow thy star, thou canst
not fail of a glorious haven.

> Dante
> Ibid. l. 55

To dream the impossible dream,
To reach the unreachable star!

> Joe Darion
> "The Impossible Dream" [1965]

Oh let us love our occupations,
Bless the squire and his relations,
Live upon our daily rations,
And always know our proper stations.

> Charles Dickens
> "The Chimes" [1844], second quarter

Keep yourself *to* yourself.

> Dickens
> *Pickwick Papers* [1836–1837], ch. 32

Honest labor bears a lovely face.

> Thomas Dekker
> *Patient Grissell* [1603], act II, sc. i

Keep up appearances whatever you do.

> Dickens
> *Martin Chuzzlewit* [1843–1844], ch. 11

We never know how high we are
Till we are called to rise
And then, if we are true to plan
Our statures touch the skies.

> Dickinson
> No. 1176 [c. 1870], st. 1

The secret of success is constancy
   to purpose.

> Benjamin Disraeli
> Speech [June 24, 1872]

I'm Nobody! Who are you?
Are you — Nobody — too?
Then there's a pair of us!
Don't tell! they'd advertise — you
   know!
How dreary — to be — Somebody!
How public — like a Frog —
To tell one's name — the livelong
   June —
To an admiring Bog!

> Emily Dickinson
> No. 288 [c. 1861]

He was fresh and full of faith that
   "something would turn up."

> Benjamin Disraeli
> *Tancred* [1847], bk. III, ch. 6

Look round the habitable world:
   how few
Know their own good, or knowing it,
   pursue.

>   Dryden
>   Juvenal, Satire X [1693]

Happy the man, and happy he
   alone,
He who can call today his own;
He who, secure within, can say,
Tomorrow, do thy worst, for I have
   liv'd today.

>   John Dryden
>   *Imitation of Horace*, bk. III, ode 29
>   [1685], l. 65

The return from your work must be
   the satisfaction which that work
   brings you and the world's need
   of that work. With that, life is
   heaven, or as near heaven as you
   can get. Without this — with
   work which you despise, which
   bores you, and which the world
   does not need — this life is hell.

>   W. E. B. Du Bois
>   To His Newborn Great-Grandson; ad-
>   dress on his ninetieth birthday [1958]

All for one, one for all, that is our
motto.

> Alexandre Dumas the Elder
> *The Three Musketeers* [1844], ch. 9

Nothing succeeds like success.

> Dumas
> *Ange Pitou* [1854], vol. I

A little work, a little play,
To keep us going — and so, good
day!
A little warmth, a little light,
Of love's bestowing — and so, good
night!
A little fun, to match the sorrow
Of each day's growing — and so,
good morrow!
A little trust that when we die
We reap our sowing! and so — good-
bye!

> George du Maurier
> *Trilby* [1894], pt. VIII

One must not always think so much
about what one should do, but
rather what one should be. Our
works do not ennoble us; but we
must ennoble our works.

> Meister Eckhart
> *Work and Being*

Genius is one percent inspiration and ninety-nine percent perspiration.

> Thomas Edison
> *Life* [1932], ch. 24

There is no substitute for hard work.

> Edison
> Ibid.

Resolved, never to do anything which I should be afraid to do if it were the last hour of my life.

> Jonathan Edwards
> *Seventy Resolutions*

There is no creature whose inward being is so strong that it is not greatly determined by what lies outside it.

> George Eliot
> *Middlemarch* [1871–1872]. Finale

To arrive where you are, to get from
    where you are not,
You must go by a way wherein there
    is no ecstasy.
In order to arrive at what you do not
    know
You must go by the way which is the
    way of ignorance.

    T. S. Eliot
    Four Quartets. East Coker [1940], III

So nigh is grandeur to our dust,
So near is God to man,
When Duty whispers low, *Thou
    must,*
The youth replies, *I can.*

    Ralph Waldo Emerson
    May-Day and Other Pieces [1867].
      Voluntaries, III

Now the laborer's task is o'er:
Now the battle day is past;
Now upon the farther shore
Lands the voyager at last.

    John Ellerton
    Hymn [1870], st. 1

Blessed are those who have no tal-
    ent!

    Emerson
    Journal. February 1850

For everything you have missed, you have gained something else; and for everything you gain, you lose something.

> Emerson
> *Essays: First Series* [1841].
> Compensation

Nothing great was ever achieved without enthusiasm.

> Emerson
> *Essays: First Series*. Circles.

This time, like all times, is a very good one, if we but know what to do with it.

> Emerson
> *The American Scholar* [1837], sec. 3

Hitch your wagon to a star.

> Emerson
> *Society and Solitude* [1870].
> Civilization

Speak the affirmative; emphasize your choice by utter ignoring of all that you reject.

> Emerson
> *Lectures and Biographical Sketches*
> [1883]. The Preacher

No sooner said than done — so acts
  your man of worth.

> Quintus Ennius
> *Annals,* bk. 9 (quoted by Priscianus)

Leave no stone unturned.

> Euripides
> *Heraclidae* [c. 482 B.C.] (quoted by
> Aristophanes, *The Wasps*)

Give the lady what she wants!

> Marshall Field
> Instruction to manager of his Chicago
> department store

To live without duties is obscene.

> Emerson
> *Lectures and Biographical Sketches.*
> Aristocracy

Practice yourself, for heaven's sake,
  in little things; and thence pro-
  ceed to greater.

> Epictetus
> *Discourses,* bk. I, ch. 18

Too much happens. . . . Man per-
  forms, engenders, so much more
  than he can or should have to
  bear. That's how he finds that he
  can bear anything. . . . That's
  what's so terrible.

> William Faulkner
> *Light in August* [1932], ch. 13

To whom nothing is given, of him can nothing be required.

Henry Fielding
Joseph Andrews [1742], bk. II, ch. 8

The test of a first-rate intelligence is the ability to hold two opposed ideas in the mind at the same time, and still retain the ability to function.

F. Scott Fitzgerald
The Crack-up

Man is so made that he can only find relaxation from one kind of labor by taking up another.

Anatole France
The Crime of Sylvestre Bonnard [1881], pt. II, ch. 4

Little strokes,
Fell great oaks.

Benjamin Franklin
Poor Richard's Almanac [1750]. August

Work as if you were to live a hundred years,
Pray as if you were to die tomorrow.

Franklin
Ibid. [1757]. May

Experience keeps a dear school, but
   fools will learn in no other.

> Franklin
> Ibid. [1743]. December

He that riseth late, must trot all
   day, and shall scarce overtake his
   business at night.

> Franklin
> Ibid. [1742]. August

God helps them that help themselves.

> Franklin
> Ibid. [1736]. June

When men are employed, they are
   best contented; for on the days
   they worked they were good-
   natured and cheerful, and, with
   the consciousness of having done
   a good day's work, they spent the
   evening jollily; but on our idle
   days they were mutinous and
   quarrelsome.

> Franklin
> *Autobiography* [1731–1759], ch. 10

It almost looks as if analysis were the third of those "impossible" professions in which one can be quite sure of unsatisfying results. The other two, much older-established, are the bringing-up of children and the government of nations.

Sigmund Freud
Analysis Terminable and Interminable
[1937]

To love and to work.

Freud
From Erik H. Erikson, *Childhood and Society* [1963]

Pressed into service means pressed out of shape.

Robert Frost
"The Self-Seeker" [1914]

We must dare to think "unthinkable" thoughts. We must learn to
explore all the options and possibilities that confront us in a com-
plex and rapidly changing world.
We must learn to welcome and
not to fear the voices of dissent.
We must dare to think about "unthinkable things" because when
things become unthinkable,
thinking stops and action becomes mindless.

William Fulbright
Speech in the Senate
[March 27, 1964]

A man of action forced into a state
of thought is unhappy until he
can get out of it.

John Galsworthy
Maid in Waiting [1931], ch. 3

The beginnings and endings of all
human undertakings are untidy,
the building of a house, the writing of a novel, the demolition of a
bridge, and, eminently, the finish
of a voyage.

Galsworthy
Over the River [1933], ch. 1

Nice work if you can get it,
And you can get it if you try.

>Ira Gershwin
>*A Damsel in Distress* [1937]. Nice
>Work

Work is love made visible. And if
you cannot work with love but
only with distaste, it is better that
you should leave your work and
sit at the gate of the temple and
take alms of those who work with
joy.

>Kahlil Gibran
>*The Prophet* [1923]. On Work

The most decisive actions of our life
. . . are most often unconsidered
actions.

>André Gide
>*Les Faux Monnayeurs* (*The Counter-
>feiters*) [1926]

The gratifying feeling that our duty
has been done.

>Sir William S. Gilbert
>*The Gondoliers* [1889], act II

When I was a lad I served a term
As office boy to an Attorney's firm.
I cleaned the windows and I swept
   the floor
And I polished up the handle of the
   big front door.
I polished up that handle so care-
   fullee
That now I am the Ruler of the
   Queen's Navee!

> Gilbert
> *H.M.S. Pinafore* [1878], act I

Man errs as long as he strives.

> Goethe
> *Faust.* The First Part [1808], Prologue
>   in Heaven

Without haste, but without rest.

> Goethe
> Motto

A useless life is an early death.

> Johann Wolfgang von Goethe
> *Iphigenia in Tauris* [1787], act I, sc. ii

Who strives always to the utmost,
For him there is salvation.

> Goethe
> Ibid. The Second Part [1832], act V.
>   Mountain Gorges.

All intelligent thoughts have already
been thought; what is necessary
is only to try to think them again.

> Goethe
> *Proverbs in Prose*

One must *be* something to be able
to *do* something.

> Goethe
> Conversation with Johann Peter Ecker-
> mann [October 20, 1828]

Man is a successful animal, that's
all.

> Remy de Gourmont
> *Promenades philosophiques*

Labor disgraces no man; unfortu-
nately you occasionally find men
disgrace labor.

> Ulysses S. Grant
> Speech at Midland International Arbi-
> tration Union, Birmingham, England
> [1877]

Somebody said that it couldn't be
done,
But he with a chuckle replied
That maybe it couldn't, but he would
be one
Who wouldn't say so till he'd tried.

> Edgar A. Guest
> "It Couldn't Be Done"

You lose more of yourself than you
   redeem
Doing the decent thing.

> Seamus Heaney
> "Station Island" [1984], XII

I am the master of my fate;
I am the captain of my soul.

> William Ernest Henley
> *Echoes* [1888], No. 4, In Memoriam
>   R. T. Hamilton Bruce ("Invictus"),
>   st. 4

The dawn speeds a man on his journey, and speeds him too in his
   work.

> Hesiod
> *Works and Days*, l. 579

Every tool carries with it the spirit
   by which it has been created.

> Werner Heisenberg
> *Physics and Philosophy* [1958]

Thursday come, and the week is
gone.

> George Herbert
> *Jacula Prudentum* [1651], no. 587

Haste maketh waste.

> John Heywood
> *Proverbs* [1546], pt. I, ch. 2

Idleness and lack of occupation
   tend — nay are dragged — to-
   wards evil.

> Hippocrates
> *Decorum,* bk. I

Life is short, the art long, opportunity fleeting, experiment treacher-
   ous, judgment difficult.

> Hippocrates
> *Aphorisms,* sec. I, 1

I find the great thing in this world is
   not so much where we stand, as
   in what direction we are moving:
   To reach the port of heaven, we
   must sail sometimes with the
   wind and sometimes against it —
   but we must sail, and not drift,
   nor lie at anchor.

> Oliver Wendell Holmes
> *The Autocrat of the Breakfast-Table*
> [1858], ch. 4

Certainty generally is illusion, and
   repose is not the destiny of man.

> Oliver Wendell Holmes, Jr.
> *The Path of the Law* [1897]

Have faith and pursue the unknown end.

>   Oliver Wendell Holmes, Jr.
>   Letter to John C. H. Wu [1924]

I think that, as life is action and passion, it is required of a man that he should share the passion and action of his time at peril of being judged not to have lived.

>   Oliver Wendell Holmes, Jr.
>   Memorial Day Address [1884]

It is said that this manifesto is more than a theory, that it was an incitement. Every idea is an incitement.

>   Oliver Wendell Holmes, Jr.
>   *Gitlow* v. *New York,* 268 U.S. 652, 673 [1925]

The riders in a race do not stop
short when they reach the goal.
There is a little finishing canter
before coming to a standstill.
There is time to hear the kind
voice of friends and to say to
one's self: "The work is done."
But just as one says that, the answer comes: "The race is over,
but the work never is done while
the power to work remains." The
canter that brings you to a standstill need not be only coming to
rest. It cannot be, while you still
live. For to live is to function.
That is all there is in living.

> Oliver Wendell Holmes, Jr.
> Radio address on his ninetieth birthday
> [March 8, 1931]

A small rock holds back a great
wave.

> Homer
> *The Odyssey,* bk. III, l. 296

It is not possible to fight beyond
your strength, even if you strive.

> Homer
> *The Iliad,* bk. XIII, l. 787

May men say, "He is far greater
than his father," when he returns
from battle.

> Homer
> Ibid. bk. VI, l. 479

Work! work! work!

> Thomas Hood
> "The Song of the Shirt" [1843], st. 2

Cease to ask what the morrow will
bring forth, and set down as gain
each day that Fortune grants.

> Horace
> *Odes,* bk. I [23 B.C.], ode ix, l. 13

To be both a speaker of words and a
doer of deeds.

> Homer
> Ibid. bk. IX, l. 443

I slept and dreamed that life was
beauty.
I woke — and found that life was
duty.

> Ellen Sturgis Hooper
> "Beauty and Duty"

Happy the man who far from schemes of business, like the early generations of mankind, works his ancestral acres with oxen of his own breeding, from all usury free.

> Horace
> *Epodes* [c. 29 B.C.], II, st. 1

He who has begun has half done. Dare to be wise; begin!

> Horace
> *Epistles,* bk. I, epistle ii, l. 40

Life grants nothing to us mortals without hard work.

> Horace
> *Satires,* bk. I [35 B.C.], satire ix, l. 59

Seize the day, put no trust in the morrow!

> Horace
> *Odes,* bk. I, ode xi, last line

All work and no play makes Jack a dull boy.

> James Howell
> *Proverbs* [1659]

It is not book learning young men need, nor instruction about this and that, but a stiffening of the vertebrae which will cause them to be loyal to a trust, to act promptly, concentrate their energies, do a thing — "carry a message to Garcia."

> Elbert Hubbard
> "A Message to Garcia" [March 1899]

Nobuddy ever fergits where he buried a hatchet.

> Frank Hubbard [Abe Martin]
> *Abe Martin's Broadcast* [1930]

A man is not idle because he is absorbed in thought. There is a visible labor and there is an invisible labor.

> Victor Hugo
> *Les Misérables* [1862]. Cosette,
> bk. VII, ch. 8

Thought is the labor of the intellect, reverie is its pleasure.

> Hugo
> Ibid. Saint Denis, bk. II, ch. 1

Avarice, the spur of industry.

> David Hume
> *Essays* [1741–1742]. Of Civil Liberty

Logical consequences are the scarecrows of fools and the beacons of wise men.

Thomas Henry Huxley
Animal Automatism [1874]

There is the greatest practical benefit in making a few failures early in life.

Huxley
On Medical Education [1870]

Oh courage . . . oh yes! If only one had that. . . . Then life might be livable, in spite of everything.

Henrik Ibsen
Hedda Gabler [1890], act II

An honest God is the noblest work of man.

Robert Green Ingersoll
The Gods [1876]

We haven't the time to take our time.

Eugène Ionesco
Exit the King (Le Roi se meurt) [1963]

My duty is to obey orders.

Thomas J. [Stonewall] Jackson
A favorite aphorism

We work in the dark — we do what we can — we give what we have. Our doubt is our passion, and our passion is our task. The rest is the madness of art.

>Henry James
>*The Middle Years* [1893]

All the higher, more penetrating ideals are revolutionary. They present themselves far less in the guise of effects of past experience than in that of probable causes of future experience.

>William James
>*The Will to Believe* [1897]. The Moral Philosopher and the Moral Life

We are spinning our own fates, good or evil, and never to be undone. Every smallest stroke of virtue or of vice leaves its never so little scar. . . . Nothing we ever do is, in strict scientific literalness, wiped out.

>William James
>*The Principles of Psychology* [1890], ch. 4

No athlete is crowned but in the
sweat of his brow.

> Saint Jerome
> Letter 14

The greatness of work is inside
man.

> Pope John Paul II
> *Easter Vigil and Other Poems* [1979].
> The Quarry, I, Material

I like work: it fascinates me. I can
sit and look at it for hours. I love
to keep it by me; the idea of getting rid of it nearly breaks my
heart.

> Jerome K. Jerome
> *Three Men in a Boat* [1889], ch. 15

I have, all my life long, been lying
till noon; yet I tell all young men,
and tell them with great sincerity,
that nobody who does not rise
early will ever do any good.

> Samuel Johnson
> From James Boswell, *Journal of a Tour
> to the Hebrides* [1785], September
> 14, 1773

I would rather be attacked than
   unnoticed. For the worst thing
   you can do to an author is to be
   silent as to his works.

> Johnson
> From Boswell, *Life of Johnson* [1791],
>   March 26, 1779

If you are idle, be not solitary; if you
   are solitary, be not idle.

> Johnson
> Ibid. October 27, 1779

Talking and eloquence are not the
   same: to speak, and to speak well,
   are two things. A fool may talk,
   but a wise man speaks.

> Ben Jonson
> *Timber; or, Discoveries Made Upon Men
>   and Matter* [1640]

Though the most be players, some
   must be spectators.

> Ben Jonson
> Ibid.

While I am alive I shall never be in such slavery as to forgo my own kindred, or forget the laws of our forefathers.

Flavius Josephus
The Wars of the Jews, bk. VI, ch. 8

"If I should die," said I to myself, "I have left no immortal work behind me — nothing to make my friends proud of my memory — but I have lov'd the principle of beauty in all things, and if I had had time I would have made myself remember'd."

John Keats
To Fanny Brawne [c. February 1820]

Without this playing with fantasy no creative work has ever yet come to birth. The debt we owe to the play of imagination is incalculable.

Carl Jung
Psychological Types [1923], ch. 1, p. 82

The imagination of a boy is healthy,
and the mature imagination of a
man is healthy; but there is a
space of life between, in which
the soul is in a ferment, the character undecided, the way of life
uncertain, the ambition thick-
sighted: thence proceeds mawk-
ishness, and the thousand bitters
which those men I speak of must
necessarily taste in going over the
following pages.

> Keats
> *Endymion* [1818], preface

There is not a fiercer hell than the
failure in a great object.

> Keats
> Ibid.

A man does what he must — in
spite of personal consequences,
in spite of obstacles and dangers
and pressures — and that is the
basis of all human morality.

> John F. Kennedy
> *Profiles in Courage* [1956], ch. 11

For men must work, and women
   must weep,
And there's little to earn and many to
   keep,
Though the harbor bar be moaning.

      Charles Kingsley
      "The Three Fishers" [1851], st. 1

When Earth's last picture is
   painted, and the tubes are twisted
   and dried,
When the oldest colors have faded,
   and the youngest critic has died,
We shall rest, and, faith, we shall
   need it — lie down for an eon or
   two,
Till the Master of All Good Work-
   men shall put us to work anew.

      Rudyard Kipling
      "When Earth's Last Picture Is Painted"
      [1892]

I am gradually approaching the pe-
riod in my life when work comes
first. . . . No longer diverted by
other emotions, I work the way a
cow grazes.

      Kaethe Kollwitz
      Diary [April 1910]

When I make a mistake it's a beaut!

Fiorello La Guardia
On an indefensible appointment

I have three treasures. Guard and
   keep them:
The first is deep love,
The second is frugality,
And the third is not to dare to be
   ahead of the world.
Because of deep love, one is coura-
   geous.
Because of frugality, one is generous.
Because of not daring to be ahead of
   the world, one becomes the leader
   of the world.

Lao-tzu
The Way of Lao-tzu, 67

Shun those studies in which the
   work that results dies with the
   worker.

Leonardo da Vinci
The Notebooks [1508–1518],
   vol. 1, ch. 1

The Future . . . something which
   everyone reaches at the rate of
   sixty minutes an hour, whatever
   he does, whoever he is.

C. S. Lewis
The Screwtape Letters [1941], 25

I've never done a single thing I've
wanted to in my whole life! I
don't know's I've accomplished
anything except just get along.

Sinclair Lewis
Babbitt [1922], ch. 34

By and large, mothers and house-
wives are the only workers who
do not have regular time off. They
are the great vacationless class.

Anne Morrow Lindbergh
Gift from the Sea [1955], ch. 3

What each man does is based not
on direct and certain knowledge,
but on pictures made by himself
or given to him. . . . The way in
which the world is imagined de-
termines at any particular moment what men will do.

Walter Lippmann
Public Opinion [1922], ch. 1, The
World Outside and the Pictures in
Our Heads

Good and evil, reward and punishment, are the only motives to a rational creature: these are the spur and reins whereby all mankind are set on work, and guided.

John Locke
Some Thoughts Concerning Education
[1693], sec. 54

No man's knowledge here can go beyond his experience.

Locke
Essay Concerning Human Understanding [1690], bk. II, ch. 1, sec. 19

His brow is wet with honest sweat,
He earns whate'er he can,
And looks the whole world in the face,
For he owes not any man.

Henry Wadsworth Longfellow
"The Village Blacksmith" [1842], st. 2

Not in the clamor of the crowded street,
Not in the shouts and plaudits of the throng,
But in ourselves, are triumph and defeat.

Longfellow
"The Poets"

Something attempted, something
   done,
Has earned a night's repose.

> Longfellow
> "The Village Blacksmith," st. 7

Blessed are the horny hands of toil!

> Lowell
> "A Glance Behind the Curtain" [1843]

They are slaves who dare not be
In the right with two or three.

> Lowell
> Ibid.

Bad work follers ye ez long's ye live.

> James Russell Lowell
> *The Biglow Papers,* Series II [1866],
> No. 2

They are slaves who fear to speak
For the fallen and the weak.

> Lowell
> "Stanzas on Freedom" [1843], st. 4

There is no better ballast for keeping the mind steady on its keel,
   and saving it from all risk of
   crankiness, than business.

> Lowell
> *Literary Essays,* vol. II [1870–1890].
> New England Two Centuries Ago

Thinking nothing done while anything remained to be done.

> Lucan
> *The Civil War,* bk. II, 657

Many strokes overthrow the tallest
oaks.

> John Lyly
> *Euphues: The Anatomy of Wit* [1579]

There comes a time in a man's life
when to get where he has to
go — if there are no doors or windows — he walks through a wall.

> Bernard Malamud
> *Rembrandt's Hat* [1972]. Man in the
> Drawer

I hope to die at my post: in the
streets or in prison.

> Rosa Luxemburg
> Letter from prison [c. 1917]

His imagination resembled the
wings of an ostrich. It enabled
him to run, though not to soar.

> Thomas Babington, Lord Macaulay
> On John Dryden [1828]

Lost, yesterday, somewhere between sunrise and sunset, two golden hours, each set with sixty diamond minutes. No reward is offered, for they are gone forever.

> Horace Mann
> Aphorism

Talk of nothing but business, and dispatch that business quickly.

> Aldus Manutius
> Placard on the door of the Aldine Press, Venice, established about 1490

"Let your occupations be few," says the sage, "if you would lead a tranquil life."

> Marcus Aureluis
> *Meditations*, IV, 24

A wrongdoer is often a man who has left something undone, not always one who has done something.

> Marcus Aurelius
> Ibid. IX, 5

Be not careless in deeds, nor confused in words, nor rambling in thought.

> Marcus Aurelius
> Ibid. VIII, 51

In the morning, when you are sluggish about getting up, let this
thought be present: "I am rising
to a man's work."

> Marcus Aurelius
> Ibid. V, 1

Nothing happens to anybody which
he is not fitted by nature to bear.

> Marcus Aurelius
> Ibid. V, 18

procrastination is the
art of keeping
up with yesterday

> Don Marquis
> *archy and mehitabel* [1927]. certain
> maxims of archy

Love the little trade which you have
learned, and be content with it.

> Marcus Aurelius
> Ibid. IV, 31

Bowed by the weight of centuries
he leans
Upon his hoe and gazes on the
ground,
The emptiness of ages in his face,
And on his back the burden of the
world.

> Edwin Markham
> "The Man with the Hoe" [1899], st. 1

Every man paddle his own canoe.

Frederick Marryat
Settlers in Canada [1844], ch. 8

I seen my opportunities and I took 'em.

George Washington Plunkitt
Definition of "honest graft." From William L. Riordan, *Plunkitt of Tammany Hall* [1905]

Men are products, expressions, reflections; they live to the extent that they coincide with their epoch, or to the extent that they differ markedly from it.

José Martí
Henry Ward Beecher [1887]

From each according to his abilities, to each according to his needs.

Karl Marx
Critique of the Gotha Program [1875]

A musician must make music, an artist must paint, a poet must write, if he is to be ultimately at peace with himself. What a man can be, he must be.

Abraham Maslow
Motivation and Personality [1954]

Among scientists are collectors, classifiers, and compulsive tidiers-up; many are detectives by temperament and many are explorers; some are artists and others artisans. There are poet-scientists and philosopher-scientists and even a few mystics.

> Sir Peter Medawar
> *The Art of the Soluble* [1967]

We only want that which is given naturally to all peoples of the world, to be masters of our own fate, only of our fate, not of others, and in cooperation and friendship with others.

> Golda Meir
> Address to Anglo-American Committee of Inquiry [March 25, 1946]

Conscience is a God to all mortals.

> Menander
> *Monostikoi* (*Single Lines*)

The superior man will not manifest either narrow-mindedness or the want of self-respect.

> Mencius
> *Works*, bk. II, 1:9.3

Conscience is the inner voice which warns us somebody may be looking.

> H. L. Mencken
> *A Mencken Chrestomathy* [1949].
> Sententiae

The difference between a moral man and a man of honor is that the latter regrets a discreditable act, even when it has worked and he has not been caught.

> Mencken
> *Prejudices, Fourth Series* [1924], ch. 11

Copy your forefathers, for work is carried out through knowledge; see, their words endure in writing. . . . Do not be evil, for patience is good; make your lasting monument in the love of you.

> The Teaching for Merikare, par. 5

This was a good week's labor.

> Thomas Middleton
> *Anything for a Quiet Life* [c. 1620],
> act V, sc. ii

All good things which exist are the fruits of originality.

> John Stuart Mill
> *On Liberty* [1859], ch. 3

My candle burns at both ends;
It will not last the night;
But, ah, my foes, and, oh, my
   friends —
It gives a lovely light.

> Edna St. Vincent Millay
> *A Few Figs from Thistles* [1920].
> First Fig

He who would not be frustrate of
   his hope to write well hereafter in
   laudable things ought himself to
   be a true poem.

> John Milton
> *Apology for Smectymnuus* [1642]

I will follow the good side right to
   the fire, but not into it if I can
   help it.

> Michel de Montaigne
> *Essays,* bk. III [1595], 1

Saying is one thing and doing is
   another.

> Montaigne
> Ibid. bk. II [1580], ch. 31

A man travels the world over in
   search of what he needs and returns home to find it.

> George Moore
> *The Brook Kerith* [1916], ch. 11

A man always has two reasons for what he does — a good one, and the real one.

> J. P. Morgan
> From Owen Wister, *Roosevelt: The Story of a Friendship* [1930]

It is not enough to do good; one must do it the right way.

> John, Viscount Morley of Blackburn
> *Rousseau* [1876]

The great business of life is to be, to do, to do without, and to depart.

> Viscount Morley
> *Address on Aphorisms* [1887]

There is only one success — to be able to spend your life in your own way.

> Christopher Morley
> *Where the Blue Begins* [1922]

No man can climb out beyond the limitations of his own character.

> Viscount Morley
> *Critical Miscellanies* [1908]. Robespierre

The reward of labor is life.

> William Morris
> *News from Nowhere* [1891], ch. 15

Push on — keep moving.

> Thomas Morton
> *A Cure for the Heartache* [1797], act II,
> sc. i

Thank God, I have done my duty.

> Horatio Nelson
> At the battle of Trafalgar, October 21,
> 1805. From Robert Southey, *Life of
> Nelson* [1813], ch. 9

O Lord, support us all the day long,
until the shadows lengthen and
the evening comes, and the busy
world is hushed, and the fever of
life is over, and our work is done.
Then in thy mercy grant us a safe
lodging, and a holy rest, and
peace at the last.

> John Henry Cardinal Newman
> Sermon [1834]. Included in the Book
> of Common Prayer

There is a knowledge which is de-
sirable, though nothing come of
it, as being of itself a treasure,
and a sufficient remuneration of
years of labor.

> Newman
> *The Idea of a University* [1873].
> Discourse V, pt. 6

A strong and well-constituted man digests his experiences (deeds and misdeeds all included) just as he digests his meats, even when he has some tough morsels to swallow.

> Friedrich Nietzsche
> *Genealogy of Morals* [1887], essay 3, aphorism 16

Even a thought, even a possibility, can shatter us and transform us.

> Nietzsche
> *Eternal Recurrence*, 30

If ye would go up high, then use your own legs! Do not get yourselves *carried* aloft; do not seat yourselves on other people's backs and heads!

> Nietzsche
> *Thus Spake Zarathustra* [1883–1891], ch. 73

Man is a rope stretched between the animal and the Superman — a rope over an abyss.

> Nietzsche
> Ibid. ch. 3

No one can draw more out of things, books included, than he already knows. A man has no ears for that to which experience has given him no access.

> Nietzsche
> *Ecce Homo* [1888]

Where I was born and where and how I have lived is unimportant. It is what I have done with where I have been that should be of interest.

> Georgia O'Keeffe
> *Georgia O'Keeffe* [1976]

Our life is at all times and before anything else the consciousness of what we can do.

> José Ortega y Gasset
> *The Revolt of the Masses* [1930], ch. 4

The masses feel that it is easy to flee from reality, when it is the most difficult thing in the world.

> Ortega y Gasset
> *The Dehumanization of Art* [1948]

Take the sum of human achievement in action, in science, in art, in literature — subtract the work of the men above forty, and while we should miss great treasures, even priceless treasures, we would practically be where we are today. . . . The effective, moving, vitalizing work of the world is done between the ages of twenty-five and forty.

> Sir William Osler
> From Harvey Cushing, *The Life of Sir William Osler* [1925], vol. I, ch. 24

Things cannot always go your way. Learn to accept in silence the minor aggravations, cultivate the gift of taciturnity and consume your own smoke with an extra draught of hard work, so that those about you may not be annoyed with the dust and soot of your complaints.

> Osler
> Ibid. ch. 22

Love yields to business. If you seek
a way out of love, be busy; you'll
be safe then.

> Ovid
> *Remedia Amoris*, 143

The wise and moral man
Shines like a fir on a hilltop,
Making money like the bee,
Who does not hurt the flower.

> The Pali Canon
> Suttapitaka. Singalavada-sutta, Digha-
> nikaya, 3:180

'Tis a lesson you should heed,
Try, try again.
If at first you don't succeed,
Try, try again.

> Thomas H. Palmer
> *Teacher's Manual* [1840]

Work expands so as to fill the time
available for its completion.

> Cyril Northcote Parkinson
> *Parkinson's Law* [1957], ch. 1

Things are always at their best in
their beginning.

> Blaise Pascal
> *Lettres provinciales* [1656–1657], no. 4

To burn always with this hard, gem-like flame, to maintain this ecstasy, is success in life.

> Pater
> Ibid.

If you don't know where you're going, you will probably end up somewhere else.

> Laurence J. Peter
> *The Peter Principle* [1969]

Not the fruit of experience, but experience itself, is the end.

> Walter Pater
> *Studies in the History of the Renaissance*
> [1873]. Conclusion

For want of me the world's course will not fail;
When all its work is done, the lie shall rot;
The truth is great, and shall prevail,
When none cares whether it prevail or not.

> Coventry Patmore
> *The Unknown Eros* [1877].
> Magna Est Veritas

The beginning is the most important part of the work.

> Plato
> *The Republic*, bk. I, 377–B

There are three arts which are concerned with all things: one which
uses, another which makes, a
third which imitates them.

> Plato
> Ibid. bk. X, 601–D

He is a fool who leaves things close
at hand to follow what is out of
reach.

> Plutarch
> *Morals.* Of Garrulity

Men, some to business, some to
pleasure take;
But ev'ry woman is at heart a rake.

> Alexander Pope
> *Moral Essays* [1731–1735]. Epistle I,
> To Mrs. M. Blount, l. 215

Let each man pass his days in that
wherein his skill is greatest.

> Sextus Propertius
> *Elegies,* II, i, 46

Follow your desire as long as you
   live and do not perform more
   than is ordered; do not lessen the
   time of following desire, for the
   wasting of time is an abomination
   to the spirit. . . . When riches are
   gained, follow desire, for riches
   will not profit if one is sluggish.

> Ptahhotpe
> *The Maxims of Ptahhotpe* [c. 2350 B.C.],
>   no. 11

Better be ignorant of a matter than
   half know it.

> Publilius Syrus
> Maxim 865

Do not turn back when you are just
   at the goal.

> Publilius Syrus
> Maxim 580

Never promise more than you can
   perform.

> Publilius Syrus
> Maxim 528

No one knows what he can do till
   he tries.

> Publilius Syrus
> Maxim 786

To do two things at once is to do neither.

Publilius Syrus
Maxim 7

There are moments when everything goes well; don't be frightened, it won't last.

Jules Renard
Journal

Win this one for the Gipper.

Knute Rockne
Attributed

Nothing can be done at once hastily and prudently.

Publilius Syrus
Maxim 557

So much is a man worth as he esteems himself.

François Rabelais
Gargantua and Pantagruel, bk. II
[1534], ch. 29

So little done — so much to do.

Cecil J. Rhodes
Last words

Think nothing done while aught remains to do.

Samuel Rogers
"Human Life" [1819], l. 49

You gain strength, courage and confidence by every experience in which you really stop to look fear in the face. You are able to say to yourself, "I lived through this horror. I can take the next thing that comes along." . . . You must do the thing you think you cannot do.

Eleanor Roosevelt
You Learn by Living [1960]

Far better it is to dare mighty things, to win glorious triumphs, even though checkered by failure, than to take rank with those poor spirits who neither enjoy much nor suffer much, because they live in the gray twilight that knows not victory nor defeat.

Theodore Roosevelt
Speech before the Hamilton Club, Chicago [April 10, 1899]

Life without industry is guilt, industry without art is brutality.

John Ruskin
Lectures on Art [1870]. III, The Relation of Art to Morals

Fanaticism consists in redoubling your efforts when you have forgotten your aim.

> George Santayana
> *The Life of Reason* [1905–1906], vol. I,
> *Reason in Common Sense*

Man can will nothing unless he has first understood that he must count on no one but himself; that he is alone, abandoned on earth in the midst of his infinite responsibilities, without help, with no other aim than the one he sets himself, with no other destiny than the one he forges for himself on this earth.

> Jean Paul Sartre
> *L'Etre et le néant* (*Being and Nothingness*) [1943]

Misspending a man's time is a kind of self-homicide.

> George Savile, Marquess of Halifax
> *Political, Moral, and Miscellaneous Reflections* [1750]

I am better than my reputation.

> Friedrich von Schiller
> *Mary Stuart* [1801], act III, sc. iv

If you want to know yourself,
Just look how others do it;
If you want to understand others,
Look into your own heart.

Schiller
Tabulae Votivae [1797]

There's no such thing as chance;
And what to us seems merest accident
Springs from the deepest source of destiny.

Schiller
The Death of Wallenstein [1798],
act II, sc. iii

Who reflects too much will accomplish little.

Schiller
Wilhelm Tell [1804], act III, sc. i

Time is man's angel.

Schiller
The Death of Wallenstein, act V, sc. xi

Do not shorten the morning by getting up late; look upon it as the quintessence of life, as to a certain extent sacred.

Arthur Schopenhauer
Counsels and Maxims, ch. 2

It is quality rather than quantity
    that matters.

> Seneca
> *Epistles*, 45, 1

You can tell the character of every
    man when you see how he re-
    ceives praise.

> Seneca
> Ibid. 52, 12

I hold the world but as the world,
    Gratiano;
A stage where every man must play a
    part,
And mine a sad one.

> William Shakespeare
> *The Merchant of Venice*, act I, sc. i,
>   l. 77

I wasted time, and now doth time
    waste me;
For now hath time made me his num-
    bering clock:
My thoughts are minutes.

> Shakespeare
> *King Richard the Second*, act V,
>   sc. v, l. 49

Men should be what they seem.

> Shakespeare
> *Othello*, act III, sc. iii, l. 126

Nothing will come of nothing.

Shakespeare
King Lear, act I, sc. i, l. 92

'Tis my vocation, Hal; 'tis no sin for a man to labor in his vocation.

Shakespeare
King Henry the Fourth, Part I, act I, sc. ii, l. 116

I am a true laborer: I earn that I eat, get that I wear, owe no man hate, envy no man's happiness, glad of other men's good, content with my harm.

Shakespeare
As You Like It, act III, sc. ii, l. 78

More matter, with less art.

Shakespeare
Hamlet, act II, sc. ii, l. 95

To business that we love we rise betime,
And go to 't with delight.

Shakespeare
Antony and Cleopatra, act IV, sc. iv, l. 20

Better three hours too soon than a minute too late.

Shakespeare
The Merry Wives of Windsor , act II, sc. ii, l. 332

Men that hazard all
Do it in hope of fair advantages:
A golden mind stoops not to shows of
dross.

> Shakespeare
> *The Merchant of Venice,* act II,
> sc. vii, l. 18

Everything happens to everybody
sooner or later if there is time
enough.

> George Bernard Shaw
> *Back to Methuselah* [1921], pt. V

Nothing contributes so much to
tranquilize the mind as a steady
purpose — a point on which the
soul may fix its intellectual eye.

> Mary Wollstonecraft Shelley
> *Frankenstein* [1818], Letter I

Liberty is the possibility of doubt-
ing, the possibility of making a
mistake, the possibility of search-
ing and experimenting, the possibility of saying "No" to any
authority — literary, artistic,
philosophic, religious, social, and
even political.

> Ignazio Silone
> Essay in *The God That Failed* [1950]

The spirit of self-help is the root of all genuine growth in the individual; and, exhibited in the lives of many, it constitutes the true source of national vigor and strength.

Samuel Smiles
Self-Help [1859]

It is not of so much consequence what you say, as how you say it. Memorable sentences are memorable on account of some single irradiating word.

Alexander Smith
Dreamthorp [1863]. On the Writing of Essays

The indefatigable pursuit of an unattainable perfection, even though it consist in nothing more than in the pounding of an old piano, is what alone gives a meaning to our life on this unavailing star.

Logan Pearsall Smith
Afterthoughts [1931]

There are two things to aim at in
    life: first, to get what you want;
    and, after that, to enjoy it. Only
    the wisest of mankind achieve the
    second.

> Logan Pearsall Smith
> Ibid.

We know nothing of tomorrow; our
    business is to be good and happy
    today.

> Sydney Smith
> *Lady Holland's Memoir* [1855],
> vol. I, ch. 12

Ah! when will this long weary day
    have end,
And lend me leave to come unto my
    love?

> Edmund Spenser
> *Epithalamion* [1595], l. 278

So long as a man imagines that he
    cannot do this or that, so long is
    he determined not to do it: and
    consequently, so long it is impos-
    sible to him that he should do it.

> Benedict Spinoza
> *Ethics* [1677], pt. III, proposition 28:
> explanation

The most remarkable thing about socialist competition is that it creates a basic change in people's view of labor, since it changes the labor from a shameful and heavy burden into a matter of honor, matter of fame, matter of valor and heroism.

> Joseph Stalin
> Speech [June 27, 1930]

Man, unlike any other thing organic or inorganic in the universe, grows beyond his work, walks up the stairs of his concepts, emerges ahead of his accomplishments.

> John Steinbeck
> *The Grapes of Wrath* [1939], ch. 14

Wealth I ask not, hope nor love,
Nor a friend to know me,
All I ask, the heaven above
And the road below me.

> Robert Louis Stevenson
> *Songs of Travel.* The Vagabond, st. 4

The Forgotten Man . . . delving away in patient industry, supporting his family, paying his taxes, casting his vote, supporting the church and the school . . . but he is the only one for whom there is no provision in the great scramble and the big divide. Such is the Forgotten Man. He works, he votes, generally he prays — but his chief business in life is to pay. . . . Who and where is the Forgotten Man in this case, who will have to pay for it all?

William Graham Sumner
Speech, "The Forgotten Man" [1883]

The day is short, the labor long, the workers are idle, and reward is great, and the Master is urgent.

Talmud
Mishna. The Wisdom of the Fathers

Oh, that it were my chief delight
To do the things I ought!
Then let me try with all my might
To mind what I am taught.

Ann and Jane Taylor
Hymns for Infant Minds [1810]. For a
Very Little Child

Theirs not to make reply,
Theirs not to reason why,
Theirs but to do and die.

> Alfred, Lord Tennyson
> "The Charge of the Light Brigade"
> [1854], st. 2

To strive, to seek, to find, and not to yield.

> Tennyson
> *Ulysses* [1842], l. 70

    Ah why
Should life all labor be?

> Tennyson
> *The Lotos-Eaters* [1832], Choric Song,
> st. 4

There is nothing so easy but that it becomes difficult when you do it reluctantly.

> Terence
> *Heauton Timoroumenos* (*The Self-Tormenter*), l. 805

To endure is greater than to dare; to
    tire out hostile fortune; to be
    daunted by no difficulty; to keep
    heart when all have lost it; to go
    through intrigue spotless; to forgo
    even ambition when the end is
    gained — who can say this is not
    greatness?

> William Makepeace Thackeray
> *The Virginians* [1857–1859], ch. 92

It is not necessary that a man
    should earn his living by the
    sweat of his brow unless he
    sweats easier than I do.

> Thoreau
> Ibid.

In the long run men hit only what
    they aim at.

> Henry David Thoreau
> *Walden* [1854], 1, Economy

Our life is frittered away by de-
    tail. . . . Simplify, simplify.

> Thoreau
> Ibid. 2, Where I Lived, and What I
> Lived For

The youth gets together his materials to build a bridge to the moon, or, perchance, a palace or temple on the earth, and, at length, the middle-aged man concludes to build a woodshed with them.

> Thoreau
> *Journal* [1906], July 14, 1852

A nihilist is a man who does not bow to any authorities, who does not take any principle on trust, no matter with what respect that principle is surrounded.

> Ivan Turgenev
> *Fathers and Sons* [1862], ch. 5

When I found I had crossed that line, I looked at my hands to see if I was the same person. There was such a glory over everything.

> Harriet Tubman
> To her biographer Sarah H. Bradford
> [c. 1868]

Always do right. This will gratify some people, and astonish the rest.

> Mark Twain
> Card sent to the Young People's Society, Greenpoint Presbyterian Church, Brooklyn [February 16, 1901]

Few things are harder to put up
with than the annoyance of a
good example.

> Twain
> *Pudd'nhead Wilson* [1894]. Pudd'nhead
> Wilson's Calendar, ch. 19

It were not best that we should all
think alike; it is difference of
opinion that makes horse-races.

> Twain
> *Pudd'nhead Wilson*. Pudd'nhead
> Wilson's Calendar, ch. 19

I believe that our Heavenly Father
invented man because he was
disappointed in the monkey.

> Twain
> Autobiographical Dictation
> [November 24, 1906]

The difference between the *almost*
right word & the *right* word is
really a large matter — it's the
difference between the lightning
bug and the lightning.

> Twain
> Letter to George Bainton
> [October 15, 1888]

Thunder is good, thunder is impressive; but it is the lightning that does the work.

> Twain
> Letter to an unidentified person
> [August 28, 1908]

Work consists of whatever a body is *obliged* to do. . . . Play consists of whatever a body is not obliged to do.

> Twain
> *The Adventures of Tom Sawyer* [1876],
> ch. 2

Your true pilot cares nothing about anything on earth but the river, and his pride in his occupation surpasses the pride of kings.

> Twain
> *Life on the Mississippi* [1883], ch. 7

We never know, believe me, when we have succeeded best.

> Miguel de Unamuno
> *Essays and Soliloquies*

Lazy people are always looking for something to do.

> Luc de Clapiers, Marquis de
> Vauvenargues
> *Réflexions et Maximes* [c. 1747],
> no. 458

Practice and thought might gradually forge many an art.

> Virgil
> Ibid. l. 133

I have laid aside business, and gone
a-fishing.

> Izaak Walton
> *The Compleat Angler* [1653–1655].
> Epistle to the Reader

All aglow is the work.

> Virgil
> *Georgics*, IV, l. 169

Work keeps us from three great
evils, boredom, vice, and poverty.

> Voltaire
> *Candide* [1759], ch. 30

What small potatoes we all are,
compared with what we might be!

> Charles Dudley Warner
> *My Summer in a Garden* [1870].
> Fifteenth Week

Give me a dozen healthy infants, well-formed, and my own specified world to bring them up in and I'll guarantee to take any one at random and train him to become any type of specialist I might select — doctor, lawyer, artist, merchant chief and, yes, even beggarman and thief, regardless of his talents, penchants, tendencies, abilities, vocations, and race of his ancestors.

John B. Watson
Behaviorism [1925], ch. 5

My rule always was to do the business of the day in the day.

Arthur Wellesley, Duke of Wellington
From Philip Henry, Earl of Stanhope,
Notes of Conversations with the Duke of Wellington [1888]. November 2, 1835

Do all the good you can,
By all the means you can,
In all the ways you can,
In all the places you can,
At all the times you can,
To all the people you can.
As long as ever you can.

John Wesley
"John Wesley's Rule"

The worst of doing one's duty was
    that it apparently unfitted one for
    doing anything else.

Wharton
The Age of Innocence [1920], ch. 34

There are two ways of spreading
    light: to be
The candle or the mirror that reflects
    it.

Edith Wharton
"Vesalius in Zante"

Commuter — one who spends his
    life
In riding to and from his wife;
A man who shaves and takes a train
And then rides back to shave again.

E. B. White
"Commuter" [1929]

Experience is the name everyone
gives to their mistakes.

> Oscar Wilde
> *Lady Windermere's Fan* [1892], act III

In this world there are only two
tragedies. One is not getting what
one wants, and the other is getting it.

> Wilde
> Ibid.

'Twixt the optimist and pessimist
The difference is droll:
The optimist sees the doughnut
But the pessimist sees the hole.

> McLandburgh Wilson
> "Optimist and Pessimist"

If a man has a talent and cannot use
it, he has failed. If he has a talent
and uses only half of it, he has
partly failed. If he has a talent
and learns somehow to use the
whole of it, he has gloriously succeeded, and won a satisfaction
and a triumph few men ever
know.

> Thomas Wolfe
> *The Web and the Rock* [1939], ch. 30

On Wall Street he and a few others — how many? — three hundred, four hundred, five
hundred? — had become pre-
cisely that . . . Masters of the
Universe.

> Tom Wolfe
> *The Bonfire of the Vanities* [1987],
> ch. 1, The Master of the Universe

The idea was to prove at every foot
of the way up that you were one
of the elected and anointed ones
who had *the right stuff* and could
move higher and higher and
even — ultimately, God willing,
one day — that you might be able
to join that special few at the very
top, that elite who had the capacity to bring tears to men's eyes,
the very Brotherhood of the Right
Stuff itself.

> Tom Wolfe
> *The Right Stuff* [1979], ch. 2

Strongest minds
Are often those of whom the noisy
world
Hears least.

> William Wordsworth
> *The Excursion* [1814], bk. I, l. 91

But I, being poor, have only my
    dreams;
I have spread my dreams under your
    feet;
Tread softly because you tread on my
    dreams.

> William Butler Yeats
> *The Wind Among the Reeds* [1899]. He
>   Wishes for the Cloths of Heaven

The intellect of man is forced to
    choose
Perfection of the life, or of the work,
And if it take the second must refuse
A heavenly mansion, raging in the
    dark.

> Yeats
> *The Winding Stair and Other Poems*
>   [1933]. The Choice, st. 1

Procrastination is the thief of time.

> Edward Young
> *Night Thoughts* [1742–1745].
>   Night I, l. 393

Strategy

Stay with the procession or you will never catch up.

> George Ade
> *Forty Modern Fables* [1901].
>   The Old-time Pedagogue

Join the union, girls, and together say *Equal Pay for Equal Work.*

> Susan B. Anthony
> *The Revolution* (woman suffrage newspaper), March 18, 1869

Even if you persuade me, you won't persuade me.

> Aristophanes
> *Plutus* [c. 388 B.C.], l. 600

Any excuse will serve a tyrant.

> Aesop
> "The Wolf and the Lamb"

Make [your employers] understand that you are in their service as workers, not as women.

> Anthony
> Ibid. October 8, 1868

The wise learn many things from their enemies.

> Aristophanes
> *Birds* [414 B.C.], l. 375

Well, back to the old drawing board.

> Peter Arno
> Caption for cartoon showing designer walking away from crashed plane

Our ideas are only intellectual instruments which we use to break into phenomena; we must change them when they have served their purpose, as we change a blunt lancet that we have used long enough.

> Claude Bernard
> *Introduction a l'étude de la médecine expérimentale* [1865]

Ask, and it shall be given you; seek, and ye shall find; knock, and it shall be opened unto you.

> The Bible
> New Testament
> Matthew 7:7

Accuse not a servant unto his master.

> Old Testament
> Proverbs 30:10

Be not overwise in doing thy business.

Apocrypha
The Wisdom of Jesus the Son of
Sirach, or Ecclesiasticus 10:26

Think in the morning. Act in the noon. Eat in the evening. Sleep in the night.

William Blake
The Marriage of Heaven and Hell
[1790–1793]. Proverbs of Hell, l. 41

Had I so interfered in behalf of the rich, the powerful, the intelligent, the so-called great, or in behalf of any of their friends . . . every man in this court would have deemed it an act worthy of reward rather than punishment.

John Brown
Last speech to the court
[November 2, 1859]

Make no little plans; they have no magic to stir man's blood.

Daniel Burnham
Attributed

Life is the art of drawing sufficient
   conclusions from insufficient
   premises.

> Samuel Butler
> *Notebooks* [1912]. Life

Without some dissimulation no
   business can be carried on at all.

> Philip Dormer Stanhope, Earl of Ches-
>   terfield
> *Letters to His Son* [1774]. May 22,
>   1749

The best of prophets of the future is
   the past.

> Lord Byron
> *Journal* [January 28, 1821]

For all men strive to grasp what
   they do not know, while none
   strive to grasp what they already
   know; and all strive to discredit
   what they do not excel in, while
   none strive to discredit what they
   do excel in. This is why there is
   chaos.

> Chuang-tzu
> *Opening Trunks; or, A Protest
>   Against Civilization*

Thou shalt not covet, but tradition
Approves all forms of competition.

> Arthur Hugh Clough
> "The Latest Decalogue" [1862], l. 19

The cautious seldom err.

> Confucius
> *The Confucian Analects*, 4:23

I leave this rule for others when I'm
dead,
Be always sure you're right — then
go ahead.

> David Crockett
> *Narrative of the Life of Colonel Crockett*
> [1834]

When you have nothing to say, say
nothing.

> Charles Caleb Colton
> *Lacon* [1820–1822], vol. I, no. 183

When we see men of worth, we
should think of equaling them;
when we see men of a contrary
character, we should turn in-
wards and examine ourselves.

> Confucius
> Ibid. 4:17

The first and great commandment
is, Don't let them scare you.

> Elmer Davis
> *But We Were Born Free* [1954], ch. 1

Beware the fury of a patient man.

> John Dryden
> *Absalom and Achitophel*, pt. I [1680],
>   l. 1005

In silence man can most readily
    preserve his integrity.

> Meister Eckhart
> *Directions for the Contemplative Life*

I assert that nothing ever comes to
    pass without a cause.

> Jonathan Edwards
> *Freedom of Will* [1754], sec. 3

Blessed is the man who, having
    nothing to say, abstains from giv-
    ing in words evidence of the fact.

> George Eliot
> *Impressions of Theophrastus Such*
>   [1879]

It's but little good you'll do
    a-watering the last year's crops.

> Eliot
> *Adam Bede* [1859], ch. 18

Prophecy is the most gratuitous
    form of error.

> Eliot
> *Middlemarch* [1871–1872], ch. 10

There's no real making amends in
this world, any more nor you can
mend a wrong subtraction by doing your addition right.

> Eliot
> *Adam Bede*, ch. 18

In skating over thin ice our safety is
in our speed.

> Ralph Waldo Emerson
> *Essays: First Series* [1841]. Prudence

Make yourself necessary to somebody.

> Emerson
> *The Conduct of Life* [1860].
> Considerations by the Way

There is always a best way of doing
everything, if it be to boil an egg.
Manners are the happy ways of
doing things.

> Emerson
> Ibid. Behavior

First say to yourself what you would
be; and then do what you have to
do.

> Epictetus
> *Discourses*, bk. III, ch. 23

The cat in gloves catches no mice.

>   Benjamin Franklin
>   *Poor Richard's Almanac* [1754].
>   February

Dare to be naive.

>   R. Buckminster Fuller
>   *Synergetics* [1975]. Moral of the Work

People who have no weaknesses are terrible; there is no way of taking advantage of them.

>   Anatole France
>   *The Crime of Sylvestre Bonnard* [1881],
>   pt. II, ch. 4

Always fall in with what you're asked to accept. Take what is given and make it over your way. My aim in life has always been to hold my own with whatever's going. Not against: with.

>   Robert Frost
>   Comment

Don't fight forces; use them.

>   Fuller
>   *Shelter* [1932]

What another would have done as well as you, do not do it. What another would have said as well as you, do not say it; written as well, do not write it. Be faithful to that which exists nowhere but in yourself — and thus make yourself indispensable.

> André Gide
> *Les Nourritures terrestres* (*Fruits of the Earth*) [1897], bk. IV. Envoi

One never goes so far as when one doesn't know where one is going.

> Johann Wolfgang von Goethe
> Letter to Karl Friedrich Zelter
> [December 3, 1812]

Things are seldom what they seem, Skim milk masquerades as cream.

> Sir William S. Gilbert
> *H.M.S. Pinafore* [1878], act II

We never do anything well till we cease to think about the manner of doing it.

> William Hazlitt
> *Sketches and Essay.* On Prejudice

Grace under pressure.

> Ernest Hemingway
> Definition of "guts." From Dorothy
>   Parker, "The Artist's Reward," in *The
>   New Yorker* [November 30, 1929]

Deceive not thy physician, confessor, nor lawyer.

> George Herbert
> *Jacula Prudentum* [1651], no. 105

Circumstances rule men; men do not rule circumstances.

> Herodotus
> *The Histories of Herodotus*, bk. VII,
>   ch. 49

It is the end that crowns us, not the fight.

> Robert Herrick
> *Hesperides* [1648], The End

If you should put even a little on a little, and should do this often, soon this too would become big.

> Hesiod
> *Works and Days*, l. 361

Observe due measure, for right timing is in all things the most important factor.

> Hesiod
> Ibid. l. 694

Two heads are better than one.

> John Heywood
> *Proverbs* [1546], pt. I, ch. 9

Many hands make light work.

> Heywood
> Ibid. ch. 5

I hold that man is in the right who is most closely in league with the future.

> Henrik Ibsen
> Letter to Georg Brandes
> [January 3, 1882]

Set the cart before the horse.

> Heywood
> Ibid. pt. II, ch. 7

The life of the law has not been logic: it has been experience.

> Oliver Wendell Holmes, Jr.
> *The Common Law* [1881], Lecture I

The concrete man has but one interest — to be right. That to him is the art of all arts, and all means are fair which help him to it.

> William James
> *The Sentiment of Rationality* [1882]

The line, often adopted by strong men in controversy, of justifying the means by the end.

> Saint Jerome
> Letter 48

Don't get mad, get even.

> Joseph P. Kennedy
> Attributed

Let us never negotiate out of fear, but let us never fear to negotiate.

> John F. Kennedy
> Inaugural address [January 20, 1961]

If you can meet with Triumph and Disaster
And treat those two impostors just the same . . .
If you can talk with crowds and keep your virtue,
Or walk with Kings — nor lose the common touch . . .
Yours is the Earth and everything that's in it,
And — which is more — you'll be a Man, my son!

> Rudyard Kipling
> *Rewards and Fairies* [1910]. If, st. 2, 4

Bite on the bullet, old man, and
    don't let them think you're afraid.

> Kipling
> *The Light That Failed* [1890–1891]

People who make no noise are dan-
    gerous.

> La Fontaine
> Ibid. bk. VIII [1678–1679], fable 23

In everything one must consider the
    end.

> Jean de La Fontaine
> *Fables*, bk. III [1668], fable 5

The best [man] is like water.
Water is good; it benefits all things
    and does not compete with them.
It dwells in [lowly] places that all dis-
    dain.
This is why it is so near to Tao.

> Lao-tzu
> *The Way of Lao-tzu*, 8

Keep strong, if possible. In any
case, keep cool. Have unlimited
patience. Never corner an opponent, and always assist him to
save his face. Put yourself in his
shoes — so as to see things
through his eyes. Avoid self-
righteousness like the devil —
nothing so self-blinding.

> Basil Henry Liddell Hart
> *Deterrent or Defense* [1960].
> Advice to Statesmen

Mishaps are like knives, that either
serve us or cut us, as we grasp
them by the blade or the handle.

> James Russell Lowell
> *Literary Essays*, vol. I [1864–1890].
> Cambridge Thirty Years Ago

Truth is generally the best vindica-
tion against slander.

> Abraham Lincoln
> Letter to Secretary Stanton, refusing to
> dismiss Postmaster-General Mont-
> gomery Blair [July 18, 1864]

Keep to moderation, keep the end
in view, follow nature.

> Lucan
> *The Civil War*, bk. II, 381

Delays breed dangers.

John Lyly
Euphues: The Anatomy of Wit [1579],
p. 65

Order and simplification are the
first steps toward the mastery of a
subject — the actual enemy is
the unknown.

Thomas Mann
The Magic Mountain [1924], ch. 5

Look to the essence of a thing,
whether it be a point of doctrine,
of practice, or of interpretation.

Marcus Aurelius
Meditations, VIII, 22

Never esteem anything as of advantage to you that will make you
break your word or lose your self-
respect.

Marcus Aurelius
Ibid. III, 7

Conceal a flaw, and the world will
imagine the worst.

Martial
Epigrams, III, 42

First ponder, then dare.

Helmuth von Moltke
Attributed

Success depends on three things:
who says it, what he says, how he
says it; and of these three things,
what he says is the least important.

> John, Viscount Morley of Blackburn
> *Recollections* [1917], vol. III, bk. 5,
> ch. 4

My doctrine is: Live that thou may-
est desire to live again — that is
thy duty — for in any case thou
wilt live again!

> Friedrich Nietzsche
> *Eternal Recurrence*, 27

Who overrefines his argument
brings himself to grief.

> Petrarch
> "To Laura in Life," canzone 11

Something must be left to chance;
nothing is sure in a sea fight beyond all others.

> Horatio Nelson
> Memorandum to the fleet, off Cadiz
> [October 9, 1805]

You will be safest in the middle.

> Ovid
> *Metamorphoses*, II, 137

A man who is always ready to believe what is told him will never
do well.

> Gaius Petronius
> *Satyricon*, sec. 43

The best plan is to profit by the folly
of others.

> Pliny the Elder
> *Natural History*, bk. XVIII, sec. 31

Perseverance is more prevailing
than violence; and many things
which cannot be overcome when
they are together, yield themselves up when taken little by
little.

> Plutarch
> *Lives*, Sertorius, sec. 16

Those who know how to win are
much more numerous than those
who know how to make proper
use of their victories.

> Polybius
> *History*, bk. X, 36

Not to go back is somewhat to advance,
And men must walk, at least, before they dance.

>Alexander Pope
>*Imitations of Horace* [1733–1738], epistle I, bk. 1, l. 53

The end must justify the means.

>Matthew Prior
>*Hans Carvel* [1700]

In every enterprise consider where you would come out.

>Publilius Syrus
>Maxim 777

It is a bad plan that admits of no modification.

>Publilius Syrus
>Maxim 469

Never thrust your own sickle into another's corn.

>Publilius Syrus
>Maxim 593

No one should be judge in his own case.

>Publilius Syrus
>Maxim 545

While we stop to think, we often miss our opportunity.

> Publilius Syrus
> Maxim 185

You should hammer your iron when it is glowing hot.

> Publilius Syrus
> Maxim 262

There was an old owl lived in an oak,
The more he heard, the less he spoke;
The less he spoke, the more he heard,
O, if men were all like that wise bird!

> *Punch*, vol. LXVIII, 155 [1875]

Never do today what you can
Put off till tomorrow.

> William Brighty Rands [Matthew
> Browne]
> *Lilliput Levee*

To get along, go along.

> Sam Rayburn
> Attributed

To succeed you must add water to your wine, until there is no more wine.

> Jules Renard
> Journal

In life, as in a football game, the
principle to follow is: Hit the line
hard.

> Theodore Roosevelt
> *The Strenuous Life: Essays and Addresses* [1900]. The American Boy

You saw his weakness, and he will
never forgive you.

> Friedrich von Schiller
> *Wilhelm Tell* [1804], act III, sc. i

Whatever is not forbidden is permitted.

> Schiller
> *Wallenstein's Camp* [1798], sc. vi

And do as adversaries do in law,
Strive mightily, but eat and drink as
friends.

> William Shakespeare
> *The Taming of the Shrew*, act I, sc. ii,
> l. 281

Delays have dangerous ends.

> Shakespeare
> *King Henry the Sixth, Part I*, act III,
> sc. ii, l. 33

Have more than thou showest,
Speak less than thou knowest,
Lend less than thou owest.

> Shakespeare
> *King Lear*, act I, sc. iv, l. 132

One man that has a mind and
knows it can always beat ten men
who haven't and don't.

> George Bernard Shaw
> *The Apple Cart* [1929], act I

You see things; and you say, "Why?"
But I dream things that never
were; and I say, "Why not?"

> Shaw
> *Back to Methuselah* [1921], pt. I, act I

They laugh that win.

> Shakespeare
> *Othello*, act IV, sc. i, l. 123

People are always blaming their
circumstances for what they are. I
don't believe in circumstances.
The people who get on in this
world are the people who get up
and look for the circumstances
they want, and, if they can't find
them, make them.

> Shaw
> *Mrs. Warren's Profession* [1893], act II

How over that same door was like-
wise writ,
Be bold, and everywhere *Be bold*.

> Edmund Spenser
> *The Faerie Queene* [1590], bk. III,
> canto 11, st. 54

Another iron door, on which was
writ,
Be not too bold.

> Spenser
> Ibid.

Men will find that they can prepare
with mutual aid far more easily
what they need, and avoid far
more easily the perils which beset
them on all sides, by united
forces.

> Benedict Spinoza
> *Ethics* [1677], pt. IV, proposition 35:
> note

Those who are believed to be most
abject and humble are usually
most ambitious and envious.

> Spinoza
> Ibid. pt. III, proposition 29: explanation

Give us grace and strength to for-
bear and to persevere. . . . Give
us courage and gaiety and the
quiet mind, spare to us our
friends, soften to us our enemies.

Robert Louis Stevenson
Prayer (on the memorial to Stevenson
in St. Giles Cathedral, Edinburgh)

The best victory is when the opponent surrenders of its own accord
before there are any actual hostil-
ities. . . . It is best to win without
fighting.

Sun-tzu
The Art of War. Planning a Siege

Victorious warriors win first and
then go to war, while defeated
warriors go to war first and then
seek to win.

Sun-tzu
Ibid. Strategic Assessments

If you pick up a starving dog and
   make him prosperous, he will not
   bite you. This is the principal
   difference between a dog and a
   man.

> Mark Twain
> *Pudd'nhead Wilson* [1894]. Pudd'nhead
>   Wilson's Calendar, ch. 16

Put all your eggs in the one basket
   and — WATCH THAT BASKET.

> Twain
> Ibid. ch. 15

When in doubt tell the truth.

> Twain
> *Following the Equator* [1897], ch. 2